GUERRILLA MARKETING
— AND —
JOINT VENTURES

out the plan for you to succeed with joint ventures. Read this book and gain the benefits of their experience!"

—**Tom Hopkins**, *New York Times* Bestselling Author of *How to Master the Art of Selling*

"Jay Conrad Levinson has given so much to the business and marketing world over the past few decades. It's a fitting tribute that his final work should focus on the power of partnering with others in business to make magic happen. This final "guerrilla marketing" title with joint venture expert, Sohail Khan, is a must read for anyone wanting to bring this magic to their business."

—**Joel Comm**, *New York Times* Bestselling Author of *Twitter Power*

"*Guerrilla Marketing and Joint Ventures* brings you the strategies you really need to team up with the right people at the right time to bring in the revenue you want to have the profitable and successful business you've earned! Destined to become a classic."

—**Kevin Hogan**, Author of *Invisible Influence*

"*Guerrilla Marketing and Joint Ventures* is a powerful, step-by-step guide that will teach you how to leverage the brilliance of marketing titan, Jay Conrad Levinson, and the world's leading Joint Venture expert, Sohail Khan. Packed full of easy to implement, high-ROI ideas and initiatives, bringing just 1% of what's taught to fruition will have a massive, positive impact on your income and your influence."

—**Steve Olsher**, *New York Times* Bestselling Author of *What Is Your WHAT?*

"Sohail and Jay hit a home run with this book. *Guerrilla Marketing and Joint Ventures* are what helped me to build several multi million dollar businesses, and Sohail nails it with his simple and easy to understand system for building profitable joint ventures. Don't walk, RUN and get this information—do what Sohail says and you will not only find success, you will also benefit fully from Jay's legacy. "

—**Stephanie Frank**, Best Selling Author of *The Accidental Millionaire*

GUERRILLA MARKETING

MARKETING

–AND–
JOINT
VENTURES

*Million Dollar Partnering Strategies
for Growing ANY Business
in ANY Economy*

JAY CONRAD LEVINSON
AND SOHAIL KHAN

NEW YORK

GUERRILLA MARKETING AND JOINT VENTURES
Million Dollar Partnering Strategies for Growing ANY Business in ANY Economy

Published in New York, New York, by Morgan James Publishing. Morgan James and The Entrepreneurial Publisher are trademarks of Morgan James, LLC. www.MorganJamesPublishing.com

The Morgan James Speakers Group can bring authors to your live event. For more information or to book an event visit The Morgan James Speakers Group at www.TheMorganJamesSpeakersGroup.com.

A FREE eBook edition is available
with the purchase of this print book

CLEARLY PRINT YOUR NAME IN THE BOX ABOVE

Instructions to claim your free eBook edition:
1. Download the BitLit app for Android or iOS
2. Write your name in UPPER CASE in the box
3. Use the BitLit app to submit a photo
4. Download your eBook to any device

ISBN 978-1-63047-156-9 paperback
ISBN 978-1-63047-157-6 eBook
ISBN 978-1-63047-158-3 hardcover
Library of Congress Control Number:
2014933868

Cover Design by:
Rachel Lopez
www.r2cdesign.com

Interior Design by:
Bonnie Bushman
bonnie@caboodlegraphics.com

In an effort to support local communities, raise awareness and funds, Morgan James Publishing donates a percentage of all book sales for the life of each book to Habitat for Humanity Peninsula and Greater Williamsburg.

Get involved today, visit
www.MorganJamesBuilds.com

To my loving wife Eva for always being there and supporting my crazy ideas, my family, my publisher, my wonderful clients, students and mentors including my Father and my dear mentor who left this world with more light than it had when he was alive, the legendary Father of Guerrilla Marketing Jay Conrad Levinson.

To you the reader of this book I thank you from the bottom of my heart for keeping the legacy of Jay and Guerrilla Marketing alive and request that as soon as you have absorbed yourself in this book to please leave a review (for others to benefit from) then go to milliondollarpartnering.com/bookreview to claim your FREE gift.

CONTENTS

INTRODUCTION

by Jay Conrad Levinson

It's almost 30 years ago that I created one of the most important marketing movements in the world, *'Guerrilla Marketing,'* which has sold over 20 million copies in 60 languages worldwide. Little has really changed in the world of business.

I've helped tens of millions of entrepreneurs, small and medium businesses level the playing field to compete effectively with the 'big guys,' and promote their businesses successfully.

However, in today's global economy more people are looking to leverage what they have or what they can, to create a successful business without having to commit their life savings or take on massive debt.

Guerrilla Marketing has always been about low cost, high impact results and out of the 200 guerrilla marketing weapons mentioned in my book the best advice I can give to small business owners is to create fusion marketing, also known as joint ventures.

In *Guerrilla Marketing and Joint Ventures*, author, speaker, consultant and entrepreneur Sohail Khan has taken this strategy further to illustrate the huge opportunities that exist in the world today to create massive business leverage for low or zero cost.

Sohail's unique skills in this area come from years of being mentored by the best (including me) and applying the strategies you are about to read in this book. In speaking about making millions, losing millions and then making a sensational comeback in just 30 days, Sohail proves that where there is a will there is always a way-- backed by taking a strategic action-orientated approach that each of us can achieve.

Many people, and you might be one of them, are looking for ways to grow their business exponentially without being drawn into the traditional 'shot-gun approach' to marketing where all they know is that they must spend money to make money. In writing *Guerrilla Marketing and Joint Ventures*, Sohail reveals Million Dollar Partnering strategies that can work for ANY business in ANY economy and combined with Guerrilla Marketing will provide your business with the most amazing marketing machine in the world.

Overall, this book isn't just about more business and marketing strategies; it's about learning and applying one of the most unique and secret business strategies that exist in the world today. *Guerrilla Marketing and Joint Ventures* also shows that when you contribute to the success of others through partnering, you win hands down. And it's not just your victory; it impacts everyone around you. You can actually create millions in your business, and when you do, everyone benefits.

PREFACE

If you are reading this book you are either a business owner looking for quick and inexpensive strategies for making big profits from your existing business OR someone who is interested in how to get everything you can out of all you have using joint ventures.

This book is based on my personal journey using the principles of 'Joint Ventures' combined with 'Guerrilla Marketing'. Guerrilla marketing principles, in particular, have had a vast influence and impact on literally millions of businesses throughout the world thanks to the teachings of my dear friend, mentor and marketing guru, Jay Conrad Levinson.

If you are an entrepreneur who wants to stay ahead of your competitors without matching their mighty marketing budgets, you need guerrilla marketing more than ever because the competition is smarter and more sophisticated and even more aggressive than it has ever been. This is not a problem for a true guerrilla.

Guerrilla marketing requires an understanding of every facet of marketing, to experiment with many of them, winnow out the losers, double up on the winners, and then use the marketing tactics and strategies that prove themselves to you again and again.

Joint ventures involve recognising the myriad opportunities out there and *leveraging every one of them through partnering*. You must seize the important opportunities, be aware of the smaller ones or overlook any minor problems. You've got to go all out; this is one of the fundamentals of successful joint ventures and deal making.

Therefore, all your marketing must be an extension of your core idea: the advertising, the joint venture partners, the stationery, the direct mailings, the telephone marketing, the package, the Internet and social media presence—the whole thing. It isn't enough to have a better idea; you need to have a focused strategy.

By reading and applying what you are about to learn in this book you will become a master of guerrilla marketing and joint ventures, the combined type of smarter marketing necessary for true entrepreneurial success worldwide in *any* economy and *any* marketplace.

Guerrilla Marketing and Joint Ventures simplifies the complexity and explains how entrepreneurs can use smarter marketing and joint ventures to generate maximum profits from minimum investments. Put another way, this book can help make your business *grow* very rapidly. This book, as you will learn, can also help an individual entrepreneur make *millions* in a very short space of time.

—PART ONE—

GUERRILLA MARKETING

CHAPTER 1

GUERRILLA MARKETING PRINCIPLES

Traditional marketing advocates destroying competition; Instead co-operate with competitors and create win-win opportunities
— **Jay Conrad Levinson**

he term 'guerrilla marketing' was first introduced by Jay Conrad Levinson when he wrote a book on this topic and named it *Guerrilla Marketing* which went on to become an international bestseller with sales of over 20 million copies worldwide. Since then, the term has become widely popular and has been used in many text books.

The main theory behind guerrilla marketing is that it employs a completely unconventional approach towards marketing and promotion, the foundation of which lies in the application of imagination, energy and time. The motive behind this new technique is to generate unique ideas that do not require much finance. The campaigns involved in guerrilla marketing theory are often interactive, unconventional, and mostly target consumers in totally unexpected places.

The main objective of guerrilla marketing is to come up with something that provokes people to think in a way that has a long-term effect on their memory while, at the same time, creating a buzz that spreads like wildfire and goes 'viral'. For example, the promoters of the cause, "Stop Nudism", played a clever and inspiring promotional campaign using guerrilla marketing when they posted their "Stop Nudism" sticker on one of the many nude female statues in London, driving the point home by covering up with a bra! This method of spreading their message was widely successful and people truly appreciated it.

In addition to such promotional stuff, guerrilla marketing also involves directly approaching customers on the streets, giving away products in malls or shopping centers in new and innovative ways, along with other PR stunts that grab the market's attention without having to spend thousands of dollars or being too over-the-top. The trick and magic of guerrilla marketing lie in innovation and creatively coming up with unique ideas. These days, the gurus of guerrilla marketing take advantage of digital and mobile technologies to gain the edge when engaging with customers and creating a brand experience for them that is truly memorable and long-lasting.

As the introducer of the 'guerrilla marketing' concept, Jay has written hundreds of books giving tips and ideas on how to perfectly implement promotional campaigns. However, it's important to stress that each company should strive to be uniquely creative in its promotional ideas thereby standing apart from the crowd and making a lasting impression on their target market. Marketers trying to adopt the theory of 'guerrilla marketing' must look deep inside their company, studying each and every little aspect of it and its line of products to find ideas for their creative promotional campaign. They have to utilize all their personal and professional contacts to take full advantage of their capabilities while spending the least possible amount of money.

According to Jay, smaller companies have more advantages and can better implement the guerrilla marketing concept than larger companies. This helps new entrepreneurs and small companies achieve widespread recognition without having to invest thousands of dollars. Small companies also have the advantage of enjoying more personal contact with their customers, giving them more options to choose from when adopting the guerrilla marketing concept. However, Jay always maintained that the most important factor in implementing the guerrilla marketing theory is that the company must "deliver the goods".

Guerrilla Marketing Principles

The following principles form the foundation of the guerrilla marketing theory:

1. This theory is specially designed keeping in view the needs and resources of entrepreneurs and smalls businesses.
2. Instead of focusing on judgment and experience as in traditional marketing methods, this theory focuses more on human psychology.
3. Unlike traditional marketing methods which mainly focus on how much money is invested in the marketing campaign, this theory focuses on imagination, energy and time.
4. This theory is based on the profit that a company makes by adopting the guerrilla marketing instead of the number of sales.
5. Marketers adopting this theory need to focus on the number of new relationships they are able to make each month.
6. The companies adopting the guerrilla marketing concept are mainly those who have a very specified and focused set of products or services that they try to excel in, rather than offering a wide range of diversified products and services.

7. The main focus of companies adopting this concept is to secure larger transactions with their current customers while increasing those transactions instead of trying to find new customers. Referrals are the main method through which they increase their customer base.

8. Companies adopting this approach do not bother about competition, trying instead to co-operate more with other companies in the same industry.

9. A great piece of advice from Jay was that companies should not only rely upon guerrilla marketing but should adopt other strategies as well.

10. Jay also advised companies to use cutting-edge technology to build their business.

11. Finally, the last piece of advice by Jay was to avoid trying to push a sale on your customer, rather always try to get his/her consent before you send any further information.

Guerrilla Marketing Today

Companies are seeing a sharp downfall in traditional marketing techniques with the average consumer constantly bombarded with around 1,600 messages on a daily basis. The traditional approach of throwing loud and flashy messages at consumers is no longer working. It seems everyone has turned a deaf ear towards all the traditional ads especially on television, radio and even billboards. The younger target audience is becoming harder to reach out to than ever before which is why companies are now turning to different techniques such as guerrilla marketing. Being flashier, louder and bigger is no longer going to work; the trick now is to turn the approach towards being more honest, intelligent, smart, catchy and different.

This is where guerrilla marketing steps in. The idea is to catch the customer in a completely unexpected setting and totally off-guard when they least expect it. You have to ensure that your campaigns are intelligent and different from the conventional stuff. Each campaign should have a certain edge to it and a hidden wisdom that can instantly click the customer and amuse them. This technique is really helping companies target their customers in a more effective manner and has proven quite successful in grabbing their attention. Guerrilla marketing doesn't involve heavy budgets or fancy settings. The normal routine setting and daily life environment are used to showcase the company's uniqueness in a way that will amuse the viewers.

The key elements involved in Guerrilla Marketing are:

Creativity

In guerrilla marketing, marketers are not bound by billboards or 15-second television slots, rather they take the whole world as their billboard on which they are free to display whatever they want, trying to come up with totally unique and unconventional ideas. So, if you want to be successful in guerrilla marketing you need true professionals with the creative knack. Creativity is the center piece of this theory.

Unexpectedness

The settings that you use for your guerrilla marketing campaign have to be totally unexpected. For example, we all expect to see a billboard while walking down a road and to see television commercials during breaks in our favorite shows. But we don't expect to suddenly be approached by someone while out shopping, or view something unusual in a park or any similar place. This is the main trick behind guerrilla marketing. When you are able to catch people off-guard with totally unexpected things they will definitely stop to take a second look and this is the best way to grab their attention.

More with Less

Another thing to keep in mind when adopting the guerrilla marketing theory is to ensure that you don't go too 'over the top' with your ideas, ending up with something completely impractical or which will be too expensive to implement. One of the main foundations of the guerrilla marketing concept is to achieve your objective with the smallest budget. Therefore, always ensure that your ideas are able to give you better results when compared to your budget. A great example of this is using *Joint Ventures*. You have to be reasonable yet intelligent when designing a guerrilla marketing campaign.

Maximize your Surroundings

When using your surroundings and environment for guerrilla marketing make sure you don't end up doing something which annoys the crowd. For example, lining the street with coffee cups or putting up a show within a heavy traffic area will bother the people passing by who may then be late due to the inconvenience you have caused them. Therefore, always ensure that you use your surroundings wisely and maximize what you have with your own creativity.

Interactivity

Relationships are an important factor with companies adopting guerrilla marketing techniques and it's important to be interactive. Most campaigns involve some sort of interaction with customers on a personal level. A best example of this would be when the furniture producing giant company, Ikea, tried to create appeal for their living room furniture by transforming a bus stop into an amazingly relaxing place and serving snacks there. This turned the bus stop into an interactive display for the Ikea furniture without disturbing the peace. In fact, people waiting for the bus to arrive enjoyed luxurious treatment and those not even waiting for the bus came over to join in the fun.

Many new terminologies have emerged in marketing that are often inter-related with guerrilla marketing. These include 'viral marketing' which mainly focuses on using social networks, 'buzz marketing' which relies on word-of-mouth advertising, 'tissue-pack marketing' which relies on hand-to-hand marketing, reverse graffiti, presence marketing which focuses on being there at the moment, grassroots marketing, astroturfing and wild posting campaigns, etc. All these ideas constitute the latest trend in marketing and promotion and are often used in connection with each other. Companies try to make the most of their resources by not relying on a single method but rather mixing and matching several different techniques and launching a promotional campaign emphasizing several different promotional mediums.

Guerrilla marketing has fast become the new wave and popular technique for designing promotional campaigns and marketing materials. Companies all over the world, regardless of their size, are shifting their techniques to more creative and unconventional ones as suggested by this theory. If firms want their target market to hear them out, if they are looking for a way to stand out from the crowd, they really need to get their creative juices flowing. Businesses can no longer survive in this overly populated and congested market place if they stick to the traditional methods of marketing and promotion. Therefore, in order to survive and compete in this stiff competition and globalized market, companies need to shift their gear towards guerrilla marketing and start thinking out of the box.

Different Types of Guerrilla Marketing

Now you know what guerrilla marketing is, you might want to learn about the various forms it takes. Find different examples of guerrilla marketing and you'll see how one can be entirely different from the others.

Alternative Marketing

This is a popular type of guerrilla marketing that uses non-traditional ways of advertising the products. General forms of marketing involve using some type of publicity statement issued by companies that are not directly to market or promote the products but to create a base appeal for these products, so that consumers are made aware of them.

Ambient Marketing

Of all the different categories of guerrilla marketing, ambient marketing tends to cost the most. In this case, you use a single thing that is most synonymous with the company and then place it in other places or things that are normally not associated with that company or product.

Astroturfing

This form of marketing is very similar to a grass-roots movement in which individuals promote a product because of the good experience they enjoyed. However, unlike the latter, which is the promotion of honest astroturfing (generally done through a blog), the people who promote products often receive payment from the company or have a company on its own. The blogger doesn't reveal they are connected to the company.

Experiential Marketing

Here, the prospective consumers are allowed to experience the products in question, so they connect with them. The idea is to enable consumers to make more informed decisions.

Think Marketing

Using this strategy, the company aims to make people aware of the presence of the product. They try to achieve this by putting the product in places where they are guaranteed recognition and exposure. Product placement in films and television shows is often regarded as a kind of marketing. On the Internet, when you place notes or photos on the different websites, you are involved in marketing.

Tissue Pack Marketing

Popularized in Japan, this form of advertising, as the name suggests, involves promoting products on the cover of tissue paper. Because it is a product that is commonly used and can be stored for a while, it is a great way to ensure that these products remain in the memory of the consumer. This technique is generally considered to be more useful than an ad in the flyer.

Undercover Marketing

Also known as stealth marketing, involves the use of celebrities to advertise products by being seen using them in a public place, the implication being they showed their loyalty to the products they are using. In this way, the celebrity's fans are encouraged to use the same products and a greater awareness of the products is created.

Viral Marketing

This kind of guerrilla marketing uses social networking sites and popular video games to build recognition of the brand and the product. This technique is such that if the commercial catches the attention of the target base, it will be released by them without the company having to issue any charges. The reason it is called viral marketing is because of comparisons that have been created with the spread of computer viruses.

Wild Posting

Unlike other more subtle methods, this form involves the over-the-top promotion of the product by placing posters wherever possible and making the message hard to miss. Of course, the cost factor here is less which makes it effective in the long term.

The Seven-Sentence Guerrilla Marketing Strategy

During our discussions Jay always stressed that no guerrilla marketing should be implemented without creating strategies with seven simple sentences:

1. **The purpose of the marketing**—the physical action you want your prospect to take, such as clicking to a web site, visiting your store, clipping a coupon, calling a toll-free number, looking for your product when shopping, taking a test drive, etc.
2. **How you'll achieve this purpose**—your competitive advantage and benefits.
3. **Your target market**—or markets.
4. **The marketing weapons you'll use** (covered in a later chapter).
5. **Your niche and your position** and what you stand for.
6. **The identity of your business.**
7. **Your budget**—which should be expressed as a percentage of your projected gross revenue.

One of the most important principles of guerrilla marketing that I have learnt from Jay is that you must be more creative than your competition in every aspect of marketing. To achieve this, make sure you create your guerrilla marketing plan properly, intelligently, clearly, creatively and consistently. Only then can you assure yourself that you are successfully marketing your product or service.

You don't have to know how to write or draw to be creative. All you have to do is supply the *creative idea*. You can always hire someone to write or draw for you, but it's not easy to hire someone to be creative about your business; that task should fall to you. Let's look at a few examples of creativity in action.

- A CPA wanted to create more business, so he wrote a tax newsletter and sent it every three months, free of charge, to a long list of prospects. By doing so, he established himself as an authority and dramatically improved his business. This wasn't an earth-shaking act of creativity, but it was an extremely successful plan. If you are a CPA or accountant reading this right now, get in touch with me for a complete twist on this idea based on my expertise as a Joint Venture Business Expert!

- A waterbed retail store wanted to cast off its counter-culture identity, so it relocated to an elegant shopping center, required its staff to dress impeccably and hired a strong, intelligent voice to serve as the announcer on its radio commercials. The results were impressive.

- A jeweler wanted to attract attention to his business during the holiday season so he invented outlandishly expensive gift ideas, such as a Frisbee with a diamond in the center, priced at $5,000. Another gift was a miniature hourglass that used real diamonds instead of sand, priced at $10,000. A third item was a jewel-encrusted backgammon set with a price tag of $50,000. The jeweler rarely sold such items but he attracted national publicity and his holiday sales sky-rocketed.

- An attorney wanted to establish warm relationships with his clients so he made it a point to walk with them from his office to the elevator, take the elevator twenty-three storeys down from the lobby with them, then walk with his clients to their car or the public transportation that would take them to their next destination. As a result, he retained a high percentage of his clients and increased his business per client.

These examples describe how to be more creative in your prospecting, store décor, employee attire and methods of gaining free publicity for your business. In the next chapter we will expand on the different types of low cost, high impact guerrilla marketing strategies you can adopt in your business straight away however, before we do that I would like to share with you an excerpt from an interview with Jay.

Interview with

JAY CONRAD LEVINSON

Sohail: Thank you Jay for your time today. Why don't you start off by talking about who you are, what you do and how Guerrilla Marketing got started?

Jay: Okay, I'll start out with what I do. What I do is marketing consultation and writing.

I started out as a secretary in an advertising agency. I got a job as a secretary because I was such a fast typist. Before that I had been in the US Army Contra-Intelligence Corp. Although that sounds exciting, and it was, the writing of the reports of investigation were the parts that excited me most which is why I tried to get a job in advertising.

I didn't have any advertising experience but they hired me as a typist. Six months later I became a copywriter.

Then I started working at advertising agencies as a copywriter in the United States and in Europe. I was finally a Vice President, Senior Creative Director at J Walter Thomson, which then was the world's largest advertising agency.

Back in 1971 I set up my own company, and since 1971 I've been working a three-day week from my own office at home. I've been writing about one book a year, most of them about marketing, most of them about guerrilla marketing, but my main messages have always been freedom and balance in your life.

When I say I work a three-day-week, I'm hoping everybody can do the same thing.

So when people ask me what I do, I always tell them I'm a typist, because that's really what I do as I write so much. But now you know who I am and what I do , and now you know how I got started.

In 1976 I wrote a book called *Earning Money without a Job*. People say, "Are you the guy who wrote the book about earning money without working?" I say, "No, you've git to work your tail off, but you don't need a standard nine to five job taking orders from somebody else."

So, that book, *Earning Money without a Job* led to me teaching a course at the University of California in Berkeley at their convention division. The course was called "Alternative to the Nine-to-Five Job."

After a few years of teaching, my students would ask me "How can you market if you have no money?" because that described my students: they had big dreams but empty pockets.

So I said, "I'll find a book for you, "but I couldn't find any such books in the early 1980's. I went to the library at the University of California; no books there. I went to Stanford University; there were no nooks there on marketing for people with limited budgets.

I went to the public libraries in Sacramento, San Francisco, and Los Angeles; there were no books. All the books on marketing were written for people who could spend $300,000 a month; not for my students. So as a service to my students I wrote *Guerrilla Marketing*.

I had no idea the book would take on a life of it's own and become available in thirty-nine languages and sell over 20 million copies... I didn't expect that.

So that's how Guerrilla Marketing came out, I wrote that as a service to my students. And then it became a vibrant, living entity of it's own. And now it's, I guess, the biggest marketing book of all time.

Sohail: That's quite an amazing story Jay. Can you explain what exactly is "guerrilla marketing" and how you came up with the name?

Jay: Well, here's how the whole thing came about: My students... many of them now are presidents of Fortune 500 companies. My students needed to market with alimited budget, and what guerrilla marketing is all about is gaining conventional goals, striving for those conventional goals but doing it in unconventional ways.

And unconventional ways means ways that don't cost you much money. Of course, you could do that now very easily with social media and email, but there was no Internet. The Internet was not a commercial enterprise in the 80's; it was only used for military applications.

So I had made a list of all the ways that I knew that small businesses could use to market. And then one day while reading the San Francisco Chronicle, I read an article by somebody and he was quoted as saying that somebody needed guerrilla marketing to make their business work.

Sohail: Really?

Jay: No kidding , I wouldn't kid you about that. Blair called me several years after the book was written and he said, "My name is Blair Newman. I know you wrote the guerrilla marketing books.

When you give talks on guerrilla marketing, who do you say invented the phrase?" And I said, "Blair, I'm honoured you're on the phone. I know that you did."

He said. "That's good. I don't mind that you use it, I just don't want you taking credit for coming up with that idea." "Oh, Blair," I said, "I always give you credit as the man who came up with the phrase 'guerrilla marketing'."

But the idea for the book was mine, and I did it strictly to help my students achieve their goals.

Sohail: Fascinating! Can you share some guerrilla marketing tactics to successfully market a business or product or service?

Jay: The tactics I'm going to tell you about cost absolutely nothing.

Sohail: Great! I love no-cost marketing strategies.

Jay: One of the most important marketing tactics is a marketing plan. Guerrilla marketing plans have only seven sentences in them.

The first sentence tells the purpose of your marketing. The second sentence tells the competitive advantages that you'll stress. The third sentence tells your target audience.

The fourth step lists the weapons that you'll be using.

The fifth sentence tells your niche in the marketplace, your position, what you stand for.

The sixth sentence tells your identity; not your image, that's phony, but your identity because that's always the truth.

The seventh sentence tells your budget expressed as a percentage of your projected gross sales. So, you tell what percentage you want to invest. That's how it starts, with a marketing plan.

Another tactic is a marketing calendar which lets you project out ahead a four year, month-by-month of what you'll be doing.

Another tactic you could use is the name of your company. About half the companies out there have very good names. The other half has bad names that confuse people or are hard to pronounce, or exaggerate or restrict expansion.

Another weapon you need to have is a theme line for your company. A theme line that summarizes what you stand for.

Your hours of operation are part of marketing, your days of operation. We're living in a 24/7 world, and that means you need to be open when it's convenient for your customers.

Another tactic is to offer flexibility. You must offer the essence of flexibility because that's what your customers hope you'll do.

Another tactic is word-of-mouth marketing, and you can get that by doing favors.

Ask yourself, "Who else do my customers patronize?" and then do a favour for those people. Example: A restaurant opened in my community. They asked themselves that question: "Who else do my customers patronize?"

The answer they came up with was hairstyling salons, so they give coupons for two free dinners to all customers of hairstyling salons within a two mile radius of the restaurant.

And the people would have dinner then come back and talk it up in their hairstyling salon. So these people got a lot of word-of-mouth marketing, but you realize, they didn't spend any money to do it.

Another tactic that should be applied because it works all the time is community involvement. The more involved you are with your community the more involved the community will be with you.

People would much rather do work and buy things from friends than from strangers, and when you become active in the community, working hard in the community, you separate yourself from strangers.

It's a very good practice to do cause-related marketing, to let people know that your business donates a portion of its profits to cleaning up the environment or curing cancer, or eliminating multiple sclerosis.

Another way that's free to market is how you answer the telephone, It's so important, how you answer the phone, people don't pay much attention to that, but the most special people on the planet are the ones who call your business.

Here are some very strong free, powerful, guerrilla marketing weapons: free consultations.

Sohail: Yes, I do free consultations or strategy sessions with prospective clients often.

Jay: Nobody wants to hear your sales pitch but many people would love a free, thirty or forty five minute consultation.

You can offer free seminars or free clinics. Again, these don't cost you anything. You can give free demonstrations of your product or service.

One of the most important things you can do is start connecting with other businesses like yours who have the same prospects and the same standards. We call that "fusion marketing".

Sohail: I call that Joint Ventures.

Jay: Yes, you see it on television when you watch a commercial and you think it's for Coca Cola, and midway through you think it's for McDonald's, and when it's over you realize all along it was for a Disney Cartoon. There's much fusion marketing going on right now.

Namely for small businesses, and on the Internet it's so easy with just trading links with other websites and people.

And how much do those things cost? They cost nothing.

Sohail: Absolutely! That is why I love joint ventures.

Jay: Your past success stories are also guerrilla marketing weapons that you should be leaning on because they cost you nothing and your prospects want to hear about the things that you've done right in the past.

Sohail: I agree. This is why I get invited to speak all over the world because of my journey and my unique success story.

Jay: Another place where small and medium sized businesses can shine over the big businesses is in the area of service. And here's what service means, only if you practice this definition of service will it work for you: Service is anything the customer wants it to be. If you have any other definition of service you're under operating.

The idea is not to take people to the state of customer satisfaction, that's easy, or even to the state of customer delight because they now expect that.

But you've got to take this to a state of customer bliss, which means you render service that's so good that people talk about it. They tell their friends about the service they're getting from you.

Another huge tactic that most people forget is follow-up. Sixty-eight percent of business lost in America is lost not due to poor service or poor quality, but due to no follow up.

Here are some more powerful weapons: You can write a column for a publication. Write it free just ask to be identified with a paragraph at the bottom.

If you don't have time to write a weekly or monthly column then write an article for publication. Same thing; they pay you nothing, but when the article gets published you get thousands of reprints or put it on your website and you are setting up yourself as the authority, the expert because you're writing about it.

Sohail: Yes, I remember I wrote an article for the popular Website Magazine about online joint ventures and had hundreds of copies in my garage to give out to clients.

Jay: Great! Also one of the most underutilized ways of marketing for no money at all is to be a speaker at a club which I know you do quite a lot of. There are many local organizations that would love for you to come in and speak for half an hour at no cost. And again, it costs you nothing.

The only true guerrilla marketing investments are really time, energy, imagination and knowledge. You don't have to invest money to practice guerrilla marketing.

If you offer your services as a speaker at a club, you'll find that you're getting a lot of credibility, much authority and people will start talking about you. It's easy these days to publish a newsletter or online blog.

Sohail: Yes, nowadays I offer my speaking services for a fee however, I have also spoken at various clubs for free as a favor.

Jay: Another tactic is to write a list of the benefits of doing business with you. The longer the list the better, then circle the main benefits, which are your competitive advantages.

If you have contact time with the customer that's longer than five minutes, that's a marketing advantage for you., It's also free for you to get public relations. If you can find something newsworthy for the PR media, that's what they need.

They need news. If you have news for them you're going to find it's not that hard to get free publicity, or you're going to be appearing as a guest on a talk show.

Sohail: I get interviewed regularly and find this is great PR for my credibility.

Jay: You can also market online. We can talk for hours about how email and social media is free and the many advantages of using both.

And the best way to market online is to direct people to your website by giving away free stuff and collecting email addresses to build your email list.

Another tactic is neatness. You don't hear of neatness in marketing courses or textbooks but the marketing plan for Disney or Nordstrom, they know that marketing of that neatness is a marketing weapon.

Another free way to do marketing is to have a referral program, which makes you realize that your greatest source of new customers is existing customers.

You should also offer opportunities to upgrade. You should have a deluxe version of whatever it is that you're selling because it costs you nothing to upgrade the sale. Another way also to market free, no cost, is to have a guarantee.

And what's the best guarantee? Is it thirty days , is it a year, is it five years? The answer is the best guarantee is a lifetime guarantee, because that will attract the most people, plus the fewest people will ask for a refund because they feel no pressure to cash in on their guarantee.

Just ask the people at LL Bean, one of the most profitable clothing stores in the world, and they offer a lifetime guarantee. Gift certificates cost you next to nothing. You can even print them up on your computer.

You'll find that brings business into your life. Sales training costs nothing. Networking costs nothing. That's when you get to meet real, honest-to-goodness prospects.

You should also consider having contests. You can have contests to get names for your mailing list. You should look into the free classified ads on the Internet. There are many free classified ads sections that are going to cost you nothing, and you'll be getting to your target audience.

Anytime you have a point to make about your marketing put it in the form of a story. People don't like to read facts but they love hearing stories, and if you use stories to tell about your facts, the reasons people should do business with you, that's not going to cost you anything.

Another tactic: Get testimonials from your satisfied customers. It costs you nothing; they'll probably be happy to give you the testimonials. Use them a lot in your marketing campaigns, on your website, social media, in your mailings, almost all over the place.

Finally, I'll mention that satisfied customers are another weapon in your marketing arsenal. There are many guerrilla marketing weapons , many of them cost you nothing.

Sohail: Wow! Jay, can you now walk us step-by-step through how to launch a guerrilla marketing attack?

Jay: I'll do one step better than that. I'll talk about ten steps to take to succeed with a guerrilla marketing attack.

Sohail: Awesome!

Jay: Anybody can launch a guerrilla marketing attack. My goal is to have everybody who pays attention to guerrilla marketing succeed with guerrilla marketing attacks, and it's a ten-step process. They're all easy until you get to the eighth one; it starts getting hard at eight.

So the first step in launching a guerrilla marketing attack and succeeding with it is research. You need information, so research your market, your product. Research the media that's available to you.

Research the competition, what they're doing; they're getting smarter everyday.

Research your industry, your prospects and your customers; see what they're like. Research the technology that's available to you. Research the benefits that you offer.

And by all means, research the Internet. Do a web search in your industry and see what other people are doing.

You'll get a lot of information during that first step of research. Now you're ready to move to the second step. That's the step: write a benefits list, a list of benefits of doing business with you.

You should make it, as I mentioned before, a long list. And once you've got that benefits list you should select or you may have to create competitive advantages.

You must have competitive advantage, they have the same benefits you offer but you may offer some things they don't. Those are your competitive advantages. That's the second step; the benefits list with the competitive advantage.

The third step is where you select the guerrilla marketing weapons you're going to use. In my book Guerrilla Marketing we list one hundred guerrilla marketing weapons.

And you can select the weapons you think will work best for you. You shouldn't be overwhelmed, because even if you pick, say, forty weapons you're not going to do them all at once.

So put them into priority order. You're not going to launch them all at the same time; you'll launch one first, one second, one third. Then put the date that you're going to launch that weapon and then write down the name of the person who's responsible for it.

Probably that will be your name, but somebody else will be in charge of that particular task to make that weapon work.

Now you've done the first three steps: the research, the benefits list and selecting weapons. Now you come to step four, we talked about it already:

Create a seven-sentence marketing plan. Seven sentences, only seven sentences because that forces you to focus.

You're not going to be wandering all over the place if you're forced to focus, so it's a seven sentence marketing plan.

And, if you show that seven-sentence marketing plan to people who work with you or to fusion marketing partners, they're going to understand what it's all about and it's not going to put them to sleep.

I've done much work with Proctor & Gamble, I consider them the most sophisticated marketing company in the world.

Proof of that is, in the United States, 97% of the homes have at least one Proctor & Gamble product in them, so that's market penetration to the highest degree. And yet for their superstar products they have seven-sentence marketing plans.

They may have hundreds of pages of documentation, but they force themselves to focus by creating a very brief marketing plan. And I told you what those seven sentences are.

Now you're ready for the fifth step: This is where you make that guerrilla marketing calendar that I mentioned before. It just needs to have twelve rows, one for each month. It needs to only have five columns.

The first column is months, that's easy, just list the months of the year.

The second column is called thrusts: What are the thrusts of your marketing that month? Were you talking about the service you offer? The product? Maybe you were having a sale? Maybe you were having free consultations? What was the thrust of your marketing?

The third column is media: What media did you use that month?

The fourth column has a dollar sign: Maybe you did spend money for marketing. If you did, how much did you invest? That's what you put in that column.

And the final column, that's where you transform yourself into a college professor and you give a grade to the month after the month is over. It gets an A, B, C, D or F. And the idea is to be honest with yourself and then next year, when you create a second marketing calendar, get rid of those things that didn't get A's or B's.

My clients tell me it takes about three years to get a perfect marketing calendar that is loaded with nothing but things that have scored an A for you. And again it costs you nothing to create a marketing calendar.

The sixth step… We've done our research, the benefits list, the weapons, then a marketing plan, then a marketing calendar. The sixth step is now to find fusion marketing partners.

Sohail: Or as I call them joint venture partners.

Jay: Yes. Find people who have the same prospects as you, the same standards as you. Find them online, find them in your community, find them at networking functions, find them at conferences you attend.

You'll find there's many people, especially on the Internet, who would love to do a fusion marketing arrangement with you, where you collaborate together. You reach twice as many people, you're reaching more people because you're collaborating with someone and cut your costs in half, because you're sharing the cost with someone else.

Sohail: And sometimes there is no cost if you do the joint venture correctly.

Jay: When you engage in a fusion marketing or joint venture relationship you're trying something that you hope will work for you, and if it does, that's great. If it doesn't you just stop and move on to the next one. If it's profitable, you'll do it again.

Then comes the seventh step: This is where you launch your attack. The way to launch your attack is in slow motion.

I'd say my average client takes about a year to a year and a half to launch a guerrilla marketing attack, so they never feel like they're in too deep or spread too thin.

Now we're down to the eighth point and this is the place where most people fall on their faces. It's when you maintain the attack. People lose more money in that area than any other because most people have false expectations about what marketing can actually do.

It's not going to be a miracle worker, it's not going to act with subtlety, it's not going to work instantly. It's going to take a while, and unless you know that you may start with a great attack because you're not getting instant results you may abandon the attack.

And I say don't abandon the attack. Stay with it because it's maintaining the attack that's really going to bring the most money into your life. And you're going to have to hang in there and remember that companies like Marlboro cigarettes, for example, the largest-selling cigarette company in the world, they invested $18 million into their marketing the first year and has brands that didn't budge.

They were the thirty first largest selling cigarette in the country at the end of the year and $18 million later they were still the thirty first largest selling cigarette in the country.

But they upheld their attack, with the cowboys and the Marlboro Country, and now they're the number one selling cigarette to men, to women in the United States and in the whole world.

The ninth step is you have to keep track, You're going to use many marketing weapons, and some of them are going to hit the center of the bull's eye. Others are going to miss the target. You've got to know which is which.

You've got to keep track, you've got to find out where all your customers come from.

You've got to find out where the visitors to your site some from. You've got to learn about them and realize that not all your guerrilla marketing weapons are going to work, but some are. And unless you keep track you won't know which is which.

Now you've done the research, the benefits list. You've selected the weapons, you've got a great marketing plan; you've got a marketing calendar; you've got several fusion marketing partners; you've launched your attack in slow motion; you know the brains and real meat of all this is in maintaining that marketing attack; you know to keep track, you can start making it sharper every week, every month.

Finally, the tenth is improve in all areas. Improve the message that you're using. Improve the media that you're using. Improve your budge, which means cut it. Improve the results, which means get more profits from your marketing investment.

If you take those ten steps, you will succeed with your guerrilla marketing attack.

It will always be improving because you know you need to improve it continually.

You'll get better and better headlines, better and better subject lines if you tweak the wording of the marketing you're using. And you'll find it starts to become a whole lot of fun and that eventually your marketing will start working.

And you'll realize that unless you put in this effort at first, to go through this ten step process, to launch a guerrilla marketing attack, you'll realize it wouldn't have succeeded. But, because you took the time to go through all ten of these steps, you'll find that marketing is way easier than you ever thought it was, and it's a whole lot more fun.

CHAPTER 2

LOW COST, HIGH IMPACT GUERRILLA MARKETING

Marketing is not an event, but a process... It has a beginning, a middle, but never an end, for it is a process
— **Jay Conrad Levinson**

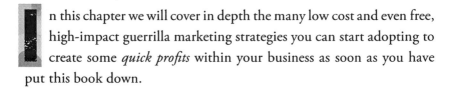 n this chapter we will cover in depth the many low cost and even free, high-impact guerrilla marketing strategies you can start adopting to create some *quick profits* within your business as soon as you have put this book down.

Business Cards
Let's begin with the obvious; almost everybody I know that runs a business has a business card of some sort. Most people include basic details on their business card such as business name, email and website, etc. However,

many people don't utilise the back of the business card, mentioning the benefits of what they offer, a strong call to action (for example, *'Download a FREE Report at...'*) or even a special offer if someone produces the card or mentions a code on the business card. **Here's a tip:** when producing a new business card leave out your contact/cell number so that when you meet people you can write it on the card. This not only looks more personal (people get really excited when I write my contact number on my card for them) but also when they take all the business cards they have gathered from networking home, yours will stand out!

Also, we now have 'QR Codes'—basically symbols that can be read by any smartphone—which direct people online to your website, social media page or special offer by people using a QR Code Reader on their smartphone. Therefore, a guerrilla business card manages to present a lot more valuable and actionable information.

Personal Letters

The writing of personal letters is not a new concept. However, a true guerrilla knows how to connect with people on a personal level and create the desired response by using this fabulous medium. With the amount of junk floating around in cyberspace, sending a personal email just doesn't work like it used to, hence the power of personal letters.

I have personally used this method to connect with people on my prospect and customer list with great success as it enables me to convey a truly personal feeling and reach a special place in the mind of the reader. You will learn throughout this book that to become a master at guerrilla marketing and joint ventures you need to learn how to connect with people, rather than sell to people. By using personal letters you can relate specific thoughts that are simply not practical in any other marketing medium, except for certain kinds of telemarketing which we will also be covering later.

To take advantage of the personal letter as a guerrilla marketing tool, remember the following:

Make it personal

Connect one-on-one with your recipient. A letter is not the same as a brochure, sales piece or Web site. Your tone should be conversational and personal but also respectful of your current relationship with the recipient. If you know the customer well, you might use humor or a more casual tone. For prospects you are just getting to know, be warm but not overly familiar.

Make it purposeful

Too often, communication with customers and prospects is generic and fails to entice a response. This "one-size-fits-all" approach does little to connect with the recipient. While this is not a time to be pushy or presumptuous, avoid being vague. Know your customer or prospect and be specific about what your product or service can do for them. Does your product or service:

- Provide a more cost-effective alternative to existing suppliers?
- Offer a way to increase store traffic?
- Streamline a process?
- Reduce waste or defects?

Build rapport

Once you have your recipient's attention, make it clear why they should consider your company's products or services. Again, what is important to this particular recipient? Look for common bonds and similarities between their company and yours. What do you have in common? Perhaps:

- Family-owned business
- Business longevity
- Experience in a particular industry
- Support of local charities

Offer an incentive

Each day that passes after receipt reduces the likelihood that the recipient will act. Make it enticing for the reader to respond. If possible, give them a reason to act now by including a time-limited offer, like:

- A special incentive or discount
- Delayed billing
- Smaller order quantities
- Point-of-purchase support
- Quick turnaround

Include a call to action

Finally, propose a next step. Remember, your goal is to build or strengthen a relationship, not just make a quick sale. So, instead of asking for a meeting, ask if you can start the relationship by delivering some form of immediate value, such as:

- A free sample of your product
- A free review or analysis
- Questions to see if your company can assist them with a current need
- Helpful information

Example of a Guerrilla Marketing Personal Letter

Below is a sample letter to use as a marketing tool for your business or organization.

Dear **(first name or Mr./Ms and last name—depends on your relationship)**

(Make it personal.) It was a pleasure to meet you at the Chamber luncheon. I enjoyed our conversation and am fascinated by

the variety of camping equipment that your company manufactures. I have fond memories of camping in the Pacific Northwest with my parents.

(Make it purposeful.) As your company continues to expand its product lines, tracking inventory will become a bigger challenge. Our accounting firm has developed a customized system for inventory control that supports multiple product lines.

(Build rapport.) We have worked with numerous growth companies that are transitioning from several products into more fully-developed product lines.

(Offer an incentive.) Through the end of the month, we are offering free staff training.

(Suggest an action.) If you are available I would like to schedule a no-cost analysis of your existing inventory control systems. This will help us identify potential future cost savings.

I will follow up with you in the next week. In the meantime, please feel free to call me at *(phone number).* I look forward to talking with you again.

Sincerely,

(Signature)

In this world of text messaging, voicemail and social networking, a letter may sound a bit old-fashioned. In reality, a well-written letter continues to be one of our most powerful guerrilla marketing tools.

Word of Mouth

In the not-too-distant past having one customer recommend you to another was seen either as a pleasant surprise or a random bonus but times have changed. We now see highly specialized agencies forming around the concept of word-of-mouth or WOM. What's more, for a guerrilla it represents one of the lowest cost promotional options of all.

According to research, 75 percent of us trust personal recommendations more than we trust advertising. Consequently, any product or service news that arrives by word-of-mouth via an acquaintance or a peer is more likely to be treated favourably and acted upon. Guerrillas have realised that instead of paying to advertise, with a prompt and using the right strategy, others could do the promoting for them.

Word-of-mouth consists of two different strategies:

1. Referral based. This aims to encourage known customers, colleagues or suppliers to give favourable recommendations about your products or services to their own contacts, thereby generating more opportunities.
2. Influencer based. This is my favourite strategy and sets out to identify selected individuals and prime them to influence potential buyer groups on your behalf but this strategy requires more specialist support.

Here is an example of the referral strategy: a firm of mortgage brokers will seek new business opportunities from recommendations given by a neighbouring firm of accountants. The accountants identify potential mortgage seekers from their own client list and suggest to those clients that they should make contact with the broker. Alternatively, the accountant will pass the clients' details to the broker who will contact them directly. Either way, the broker will probably offer the accountant some kind of reward incentive for their efforts and to encourage future referrals.

5 Steps To A Perfect Referral Strategy:

1. Set a target—how many referrals do you want per week or per month?
2. Identify satisfied customers who are likely to refer you.

3. Ask actively and specifically for the referral or referrals.
4. Confirm the approach—will they contact them or hand them over to you?
5. Measure the outcome against your targets.

Here is an example of the influencer strategy:– preparing for the launch of a new feminine product, a small pharmaceutical company identified 50 influencers who were representative of the target audience and willing to attend a pre-launch event. Free samples were distributed for the influencers to share with friends and contacts. A second event was arranged and the influencers were asked to attend and, this time, to bring a friend. Lifestyle and female media professionals were also invited, along with a celebrity host. By repeating this in several locations the small pharmaceutical company ensured that thousands of customers were primed and favourably familiar with their product by the launch date.

5 Steps To A Perfect Influencer Strategy

1. Identify the influencers—those with the potential to influence buyers.
2. Set targets for the number of buyers you want and the number of influencers needed.
3. Market to the influencers—give them a reason to be interested in you and your message. (I cover how to connect with influencers in a later chapter.)
4. Market through the influencers—give them tools to carry out your message.
5. Measure the outcome against targets.

Telemarketing

Telephone marketing or telemarketing simply means utilising the phone to call or consult your hottest prospects. A fellow guerrilla and someone whom I've had the pleasure of meeting, Chet Holmes, refers to this list as your 'Dream 100'—the 100 clients you'd most like to acquire. He recommends a laser focus on getting their business, not immediately but eventually through building a long-term connection.

Guerrillas use telemarketing to make their ads and other marketing efforts work harder. They know that 7 percent of people hang up on all telemarketers, that 42 percent hang up on some telemarketers, and that 51 percent listen to all telemarketers.

So, here is what you do. You run an ad. You ask readers to call you, using your toll-free number (unless you're advertising to people outside your area code), and then you sell them right there on the telephone. If you're doing that kind of telemarketing now, and you're not using a script, you're not taking telemarketing as seriously as you ought to. Telemarketing surpassed direct mail a long time ago, and since that time, five crucial points have been discovered and followed by guerrillas.

These are the five simple things you should do to match them:

1. **Find out** who are your top three telemarketers.
2. **Make** an audio recording of those top three people.
3. **Create** a script, using the words, phrases and voice inflections of the top three. In that script, underline the phrases stressed by these top producers.
4. **Distribute** copies of the three recordings plus three scripts to go with them. Give a set to each of your other telemarketers.
5. **Ask** those other telemarketers to memorize the script and get it down so pat that it sounds as though it's delivered straight from the heart.

It's okay for the telemarketers to eliminate any words that seem uncomfortable to them, substituting another word. However, they should not get rid of any words and phrases that all three top producers are using.

Okay, now you've got your script. How do you make it work wonders? First, recognize that you must deliver the words on that script to the right audience; that's a full 40% of your success equation. It comes ahead of everything else. Since the people calling you have responded to your ad, there's a good chance they are the right audience when they call which gives you a lot of momentum.

The right offer is the second 40% of your equation. It tells about the benefits you offer, your company, your product or service, and includes how you present your offering.

The right creative approach to a telemarketing script includes the actual words and phrases that will be used. This is the last 20% of your success equation. The right audience and the right offer are considerably more important than the right words. Still, the script you use can make the difference between mild success and wild success. What about that script?

Start by realizing that it has three parts. The introduction is where you introduce yourself by name and begin to establish rapport. The body is where you present the logical (for the left-brained callers) and the emotional (for the right-brained callers) reasons that they should buy right now. The close is where you ask the person to respond positively to your offer. Be sure, when creating your script that you know:

- **What the caller should do after hearing the message.**
- **Whether the caller should order using a credit card.**
- **Whether the caller should send for your brochure.**

People are more powerfully motivated by security needs than almost anything else. In direct marketing, you give that security by offering a guarantee or a trial offer. Are these really necessary? Yes, they're crucial!

Your introduction is the most important part of your script, even though it's the second impression that you will make, the ad being the first. Remember that the introduction is the headline of your message and that the headline is the real name of the game. The close should be written next because it's your final goal. The body should be created last so that it leads right into the close. Edit it mercilessly, making sure every word and phrase adds to the effectiveness of your introduction. If not, scrap them.

Yes, you should ask questions. Yes, you should respond to the answers. Yes, you should read over your opening line and see if it would excite you as a caller. Questions you might ask at the close include:

- **Are these the results you want for yourself or your company?**
- **Shall we get started?**
- **May I sign you up now?**

I know that it's tough to operate from a script if you're a free spirit. But I also know that free spirits fail dismally at telemarketing. I've witnessed several tests of scripts versus outlines and the scripts win every time. The winning combination for guerrillas is a potent ad, followed by a potent script so they win sales, relationships, customers' hearts, and profits.

Joint Ventures

This of course, is my favourite guerrilla marketing strategy and one that I have personally used to make MILLIONS! The key to successful guerrilla marketing is in embracing not the concept of competition, but the beauty and advantage of co-operation.

One of the most rewarding, inexpensive, under-utilized and effective methods of marketing is to tie-in your marketing efforts with the efforts of others. In the US this used to be known as "tie-ins." A Business Week cover article referred to it as "Collaborative Marketing". In Japan and by guerrillas worldwide, this make-everybody-wealthy marketing tactic is called "fusion marketing" or "joint ventures."

The best and most well-known example of a joint venture is when one company endorses (recommends) someone else's product or services to their customer list and both share the additional profits. This is a win/win arrangement!

Joint venture marketing is the guerrilla saying, "Hey Emily, if you enclose my brochure in your next mailing, I'll enclose your brochure in mine." "Peter, put up a sign for my store in your business; I'll put up a sign for your business in my store."

Emily and Peter immediately see the wisdom in the guerrilla's offer. Their marketing exposure has just been expanded. Their marketing costs have just been reduced. Hey, this is a good idea! Of course it is! Why do you think you're watching all those McDonald's commercials which turn into Coca-Cola commercials and end up as Hasbro commercials? Why do you think so many members of frequent flier clubs have learned that their airlines have fused with hotel chains, auto rental companies, even cruise lines? Because there's a whole lot of fusing going on!

It's happening very visibly among large businesses, but it's now happening more frequently among small businesses. The gas station fuses with the video store. The restaurant fuses with the clothing store. The sporting goods store fuses with the ski area AND the tennis club AND the golf course. It's happening all over!

Many organizations that have leads know that other organizations, marketing different things, have the SAME kinds of leads. So what do guerrilla organizations do? They form 'leads clubs. At the end of each month, they trade leads. Who wins? EVERYONE. Who loses? Nobody. That's why joint ventures are such a HAPPENING guerrilla marketing tactic.

The purpose of a joint venture arrangement is mutual profitability; glad we're clear on that one. Realize that almost everyone in your community is a potential joint venture partner and that almost all of them will see the wisdom in your suggestion of a tie-in together. Once you do a joint venture, you'll see the utter simplicity of SPREADING your marketing wings while REDUCING your marketing costs.

Yellow Pages

You will be surprised how many people still use the Yellow Pages and what advantages they can reveal to a guerrilla. Where it used to be easy to reach your intended consumer through a small number of media channels, there are now many options for a small business advertiser. Yellow Pages companies have responded by introducing new offerings that leverage these areas of growth, while also working to preserve and enhance print and other existing offerings that have and continue to drive leads for millions of businesses across the country.

The first thing you should do is decide whether your business can actually benefit from Yellow Pages marketing. Will people look there to find a product or a service such as yours? If you are a retailer, the chances are that people will consult the Yellow Pages phone directory and find out about you. However, if you are an artist or a consultant, people will probably find out about you through other sources.

Without a doubt, the Yellow Pages space is in a state of transformation. Research has found that fewer people are using print directories in both numbers and frequency than they have previously, and a multitude of new platforms ranging from the Web and mobile directories to iPhone and iPad apps and daily deals offerings are fragmenting the way consumers make purchasing decisions.

The great thing with using the electronic pages is that, as a guerrilla, you can test and measure direct response from ads and change them regularly to get the desired effect which is not possible with print ads.

Yellow Pages providers have completely changed their playbooks. Company names and business strategies have changed to reflect a new era in which they use their experience in the local advertising space to deliver a full-spectrum of local marketing services to neighborhood businesses.

Many people would be surprised to learn that the same companies that deliver their phonebooks also provide them with the local business information they find online or access via apps on their mobile device, or the daily deals they purchase through links shared on social networks like Facebook and Twitter.

Local businesses might be intrigued to hear that the company that publishes their local directory also offers advice on areas like SEO, paid search, online advertising, online reputation and social media. Yellow Pages providers are often behind vertical websites dedicated to selling cars or wedding planning.

As BIA/Kelsey's recent update of its Global Yellow Pages report indicated, newer Yellow Pages offerings like websites, video, social, mobile and search engine marketing will be their primary growth drivers in the coming years. And by 2015, an estimated 53% of Global Yellow Pages revenues will be digital, compared with 29% in 2011. Yellow Pages providers should be judged on everything they are doing and will be doing in the near future to drive growth.

If you plan to use Yellow Pages marketing, here are some guerrilla tips:

- Do list a whole lot of facts about yourself.
- Do treat it like a personal communication, not a cold listing.
- Do let people know whether you accept credit cards or can finance.
- Do gain the reader's attention with a strong headline.
- Do let people know all the reasons they should buy from you.
- Don't let the Yellow Pages people write your ad.
- Don't allow your ad to look or sound boring.
- Don't fail to include your website or social media sites in your ad.

If there are several pages of Yellow Pages listings for your competitors which is often the case, you can copy the strategy of a chiropractic guerrilla who was in the same situation. There were five pages of ads where he wanted to run his. So, he ran a smallish ad, clear yellow type reversed out of a black background. The copy read:

**FREE TELEPHONE CONSULTATION
ON HOW TO SELECT A CHIROPRACTOR
CALL 1-800-000-0000**

Looking at the ad above, I can tell you that he ended up getting the lion's share of the phone calls and nearly ALL the business.

Classified Ads

I bet when you think of classified ads you think in terms of finding a job, looking for a car, selling a sofa, buying a boat or locating a house or apartment. Well think again. Classified advertising can also be used to support and grow a business.

I absolutely love classified ads and this is how I built and grew my first 8-figure business. Classified advertising has been around for probably 400 years (or more). If I remember rightly, some of the first classified ads were in English newspapers (so I guess we can take the credit for that!).

A classified ad is really just a brief description of something someone is offering in the hope that somebody else is going to be interested in it. Let's get more specific. A classified ad is really a brief description of a product or service that you are offering. Seems simple enough.

The problem lies in the word "brief". Unless you have a $1,000,000 advertising budget, most of your classified ads are going to be less than 50 words, (sometimes less than 25).

You can find places that will let you place 100 word classified ads but they are either going to be too expensive or you wouldn't want your ad there in the first place. There isn't anything wrong with cheap classified ads but most of them aren't going to have any pull and you are going to have to place a lot of them to make any money.

You want to shoot for a five-fold return on all your classified advertising. If you spend $50 on an ad, it should bring in $250 worth of front-end business. If you spend $1,000 in 16 big Sunday newspapers, you should aim to get $5,000 in book orders or sales of services or products.

There are plenty of things that you can do to ensure that classified ads work for you. Before I cover how to create a guerrilla classified ad, let me show you how I started my first company from scratch using classified ads and built it to 8-figures using a unique combination of classified ads and joint ventures. I still remember the first classified ad I placed in The London Evening Standard which was targeted at people commuting to and from work; this was the ideal customer for our computer training certification programs. We ran a smallish ad, clear black type reversed out of a white background. The copy read:

SAVE OVER $3,000 ON IT CERTIFICATION
FOR A FREE 'NO OBLIGATION' BROCHURE
CALL 1-800-000-1234

The whole idea behind this ad was to prompt a direct response from the reader tired from his normal dead-end job, who would request a FREE brochure. Our first ad came out on a Tuesday and by Thursday we had over 500 requests for brochures and from that one ad fulfilled 52 orders at $785 each (making $40,820 in sales from a $150 classified ad) for our home study certification kits.

Times have since changed over the last few years and, with the introduction of the Internet, competition is very fierce. Amongst the fastest-growing segments of classified ads are those appearing online, many of which are free. Generally, you can now run classified ads in magazines, daily or weekly newspapers, classified-only newspapers and online.

Creating a Guerrilla Classified Ad

To beat the competition, guerrillas need to think differently. Let's list some of the things that you should and shouldn't do with your ads.

What you do want to do

1. Get people interested with a mini headline.
2. Get people to read the ad.
3. Get them to take some sort of action.

What you don't want to do

- Do not try and sell the entire product in your ad (if possible).
- List your price (unless you are selling a commodity or it is a selling point).

The Three Parts to a Successful Guerrilla Classified Ad

Let's go over all three to see how you can create the hottest ads around.

1. The headline (capture their interest).
2. The body (get them to read).
3. The action (what you want them to do).

The Headline

Your goal with your headline is to get the reader to notice your ad and read the body, which contains the real information about what you are offering. I like headlines that grab people's attention like:

"Earn a lucrative lifestyle with your own unique joint venture brokering business."

"The diet pill so incredibly hot you will even lose weight while you sleep."

Use short words and phrases that will get people's attention, such as, 'How to', 'The secrets of', 'What is wrong with', 'Which', 'Why you never want to' and 'The best'. Don't forget the three words that people love…FREE, DISCOUNTED and SAVE (or savings). Those three words have probably accounted for billions in sales of all sorts of products.

The only time that I like to use the word "free" is if I am trying to give away a free report or free cd/dvd that will eventually sell them a product.

The Body

In a larger ad, the body will account for much of what you are going to say. In a classified ad, it's different in that it is going to give some basic information or an idea of what you are going to give the customer. "xxx xxxxx xx xxxx xx x xxxxxx xxxxxx- Joint Venture Expert Sohail Khan is looking for like-minded professional people to join him and build a lucrative lifestyle as a Certified Joint Venture Broker. xxx (xxx) xxx-xxxx xx xxxxxx xx xxxxxx xxx.xxxxxxx.xxx"

It is really the meat of the classified. The headline and what you want them to do are the bread. The headline is the attention grabber and the end states the action you want them to take but the body is the most important section.

The Action

OK, finally if we are trying to get the reader to do something, what are our realistic choices? Quite simply, from our classified ad we want them to take one of 3 actions:

1. **To get them to come to your website.**
2. **Get them to call an 800 number.**
3. **Get them to e-mail you for more information.**

What you don't want to do is have them:
- Contact you by mail (unless this is one of the options).
- Call a long distance phone number.

Fliers and Brochures

Fliers
A flier is considered by many guerrillas to be the purest of weapons. It gets instant action if used properly. It is astonishingly inexpensive, especially if produced on your own computer; it lets you use color in a sea of black and white and it's the essence of simplicity and flexibility if you do it right. Your flier should:

- Make a clear and persuasive offer.
- Have an element of urgency.
- Get right to the point.
- Tell the prospect what to do next.
- Tie-in with your current identity

The simplest form of flier is a single sheet of paper, printed on one side. Printing on both sides makes a booklet or brochure which we will cover later. When writing a flier, think first of the basic idea you wish to express, then try to match a picture (art or photograph) to a set of words. After you've stated your idea as briefly as possible, try to explain more fully what you are offering. *Always* be sure to include relevant information such as your address and phone number. A flier is a headline. In fact, many guerrillas regard a flier as *all headline*.

Let's explore an example; an entrepreneurial-minded contractor who calls himself Handyman Hank. Hank markets his services well and has decided to improve business by distributing a flier. This is how he should proceed.

He first uses a flier to see how this marketing vehicle would work for him. If it works well, he might upgrade it to a brochure. On the flier, he includes a drawing of a man (himself) doing five tasks at the same time in front of a house. Above the drawing, he lists his company name which, incidentally, makes a great headline for his flier: "**IT'S HANDYMAN HANK!**" Beneath that headline and picture, he briefly states his offering:

He builds sun decks and patios.

He installs skylights and hot tubs.

He paints and puts up wallpaper.

He does masonry and electric work.

He also designs and makes building plans.

HANDYMAN HANK DOES IT ALL!

Call him at 858-8686 anytime, any day.

All work guaranteed. Contractor's License #34-34562

A very simple flier. The cost for Handyman Hank to write the flier was nil. An art student drew the illustration for $5 and was found on a website that I and other guerrillas in the know frequently use called http://www.fiver.com. The cost to produce 5,000 fliers, including paper, was another $100. So he spent a total of $105, which works out at four cents per flier.

Thousand, places one thousand on auto windshields (with the help of a hired high school student), distributes one thousand at a home show in his area, hands out one thousand at a local flea market Handyman Hank then distributes his fliers by several methods. He mails one and keeps one thousand to give to satisfied customers to pass on to their friends and neighbours.

Another thing the enterprising handyman also did was to ask each of his customers where they had heard of him. When they said, "I saws your flier." he asked where they had seen it. By doing so, he learned which of the five methods of flier distribution was most effective. That's guerrilla marketing in a nutshell! Not expensive but very effective.

Brochures

To plan a successful brochure for any purpose, you have to ask yourself what the brochure is specifically supposed to do for you. Get leads? Close sales? Generate phone calls? Web site visits? Electronic and printed brochures are expensive. So don't say anything you'll want to amend within a year! Following up on everyone who requests any kind of brochure is the key to success.

So back to our earlier example of 'Handyman Hank', I guess he would plan to use the same drawing on the cover that he used on his flier. After all, if it worked once, it should work again. It also makes good economic sense to repurpose what you already have. His cover would show his drawing, list his company name and maybe list the other copy point from his original flier. Guerrillas realize that the real purpose of the cover is to give people a reason to read the rest of the brochure. Again, the cover should go a long way towards answering the prospect's most important question and something I not only ascribe to but also teach ALL my students and clients: "What's in it for me?"

Now his second page should list pertinent information about Handyman Hank such as his experience, training, skills, offerings and the jobs he has accomplished. It might even include a photo of him. The purpose of this page? To build his credibility. As a guerrilla, he knows that the more credible he is, the better the results he will derive from his marketing.

Page 3 might show photos of a sun deck and a patio and would give a description, about five sentences long, of the Handyman's capabilities in this area. Page 4 would show photos of a skylight and a hot tub that he installed. Again, five or six sentences would indicate his expertise. Page 5 might show photos of a room that Handyman Hank painted and another room that he papered. It would also include some copy attesting to his talent at painting and papering.

Page 6 could feature photos of houses with masonry and electrical work he's successfully undertaken, including both an exterior and interior shot. Again, copy would describe the work accomplished. Each of these pages should repeat the short copy lines from the cover. For example, the seventh page, carrying a photograph of a gorgeous room addition that he designed and built, would carry the headline, "Handyman Hank also makes building plans and building designs." A few sentences of copy would follow the photo. Remember, the purpose of the brochure is to *inform*.

Finally, his eighth page, the back cover, would provide the name of his company, his phone number, fax number, web site, Facebook fan page address, e-mail address, contractor's license number and a copy of the nest photo from the interior of the brochure. Such a brochure may cost as much as one dollar or more per unit. It's worth it, considering his profit per sale. He runs a relatively simple business, so his brochure is focused. If he had other special offerings, such as stained glass windows, he'd create separate brochures for those talents.

If you are looking to produce fliers or brochures, be sure to tell people exactly what you'd like them to do—should they call you, visit you, visit your web site, fax you or send you e-mail? You will be surprised how many fliers and brochures I come across which, after reading them, leave me with no clue what to do next? So, make sure you tell prospects exactly what you want them to do next because guerrillas assume nothing and test everything!

Remember earlier I spoke about giving away a free brochure to prospects in a classified ad then getting them to act by placing an order from the brochure? The whole idea behind this ad was to prompt a direct response from the reader tired from his normal dead-end job, who would request a FREE brochure. Our first ad came out on a Tuesday and by Thursday we had over 500 requests for brochures and from that one ad fulfilled 52 orders at $785 each (making $40,820 in sales from a $150 classified ad) for our home study certification kits.

Now, when people call or write requesting your free brochure, also send them a brief handwritten or signed note thanking them for taking the time to request it. Then follow up with a phone call, card or a letter within ten days. If you do this, you can expect between 25% and 33% of brochure requests to convert to paying customers.

Gift Certificates

Gift certificates are no longer the domain of department stores as more and more marketing guerrillas are learning that gift certificates work in virtually any business, especially those in which gift certificates have never previously been offered.

Gift certificates are a great way to make more sales and increase customer loyalty for your business. The reason is that offering gift certificates plants the idea in the minds of your prospects and their friends. When it comes to giving a gift, people are always on the lookout for new ideas.

Gift certificates work. They help you make more sales by reaching new customers, and they will also increase your sales for other reasons: indeed, most customers will spend more than the face value of the card (on average, 20% more). A minority (about 10%) will use only part of the certificate's value, which means you keep the profit.

When someone buys a gift certificate, they are pre-paying you for services that another person will receive later. In other words, gift certificate sales really represent cash deposits or full payments for services planned for the future, which means 100% of the cash is yours to use until the certificate is redeemed.

Gift certificates provide the opportunity to advertise and promote your business with wallet-sized billboards. You were paid on the sale of the gift certificates, so you are allowing new customers to try out your business with a paid visit from your existing customers.

Your gift certificate marketing strategy should target the following objectives:

- Communicating the fact that gift certificates are available and are a popular and desirable gift.
- Conveying the relevance, variety and quality of the gift certificate; offer upsells such as metal tins, boxes and die-cut envelopes for a distinctive touch and to add to the fun.
- Reinforcing the "convenience" benefit of purchasing gift certificates.
- Building awareness of your gift certificate program through inclusion of certificates in print, direct mail, e-mail, online, and other advertising opportunities.

You should place all gift certificate designs on a highly visible, easily accessible, well-organized page on your website, as well as on your confirmations and receipts, which will appeal to impulse purchasers. Big stores all have their gift cards at that location, because it works.

A very effective way to market your gift certificates is to partner with another local business. The way it works is that you offer gift certificates for the other business, and they would do the same. It works better if your businesses are somehow related, or could attract the same category of customer.

Gift certificates are usually given for special occasions such as a birthday, Christmas, graduation, etc. Make sure that you have a wide array of gift certificates so that you can accommodate all gifting desires. Having unique designs and personalization options like space to write a personal message helps. You can also have designs that appeal to corporate customers, so that you don't miss potential sales.

Reciprocal agreement is a widely used sales technique meaning that you first give an item to somebody. The sense of reciprocation, deeply rooted in human social behavior, makes the customer want to give something back. You could offer a gift certificate of small value to a person visiting your shop for the first time. Reciprocal agreement kicks in and you have turned a visitor into a customer, likely along with a juicy purchase.

Public Relations and Press Releases

'Public relations' means exactly what it says. It's also accurate to say that it means publicity—free stories and news about you and/ or your company in newspapers, magazines, newsletters, on radio and TV, and in any other media. It means *any* relationship you have with *anybody*. In fact, the purest form of public relations is *human* relations.

Here's what is good about publicity—it's free. It is very believable. It gives you and your company a lot of credibility and stature. It helps establish the identity of your business and gives you authority. It is read by a large number of people. It is remembered.

Many entrepreneurs feel that there is no such thing as bad publicity; that as long as you get your name out there before the public, that's fine. But most guerrillas know that bad publicity leads to negative word-of-mouth marketing, known to spread faster than wildfire. Bad publicity is bad. Good publicity is great.

Public relations can be targeted at a specific audience. This is done firstly by identifying the target group, then identifying the media most likely to reach that group and, finally, by ensuring that the news released is relevant to both. If news is to be sent to a variety of media contacts it is wise to adapt the first paragraph to appeal to the special interests of each contact, if possible.

Here's an example of public relations in action: a manufacturer of motorised luxury golf carts became the sole US stockist of high quality Italian components. This provided five public relations opportunities. Firstly, the news was released to the trade press at a champagne reception held during a trade exhibition. Secondly, the news was celebrated in the staff newsletter and then featured in the local press because of its potential to support employment opportunities. The company's existing customers each received a personal letter informing them of the announcement and finally the news was uploaded to the company's online news archive to be available to website visitors. One piece of news—five different ways of using it.

Arguably the most common PR tool is *the press release*. A press release must be interesting and well written enough to appeal to the journalist first. Reporters, news editors and editors are the gatekeepers of a publication. If they don't like it, they won't print it. Make your first paragraph strong—cover the '*who, what, when, where, why and how*' details keeping it short and sharp; if the news is exciting let your enthusiasm come through. Include your contact details and be available for questions.

As you know, I'm all about being connected and building my million dollar rolodex on a regular basis. One of your tasks as a guerrilla is to get the same kind of rolodex and to include PR pros within that. The more publicity contacts you have, the more free publicity you'll generate; it's that simple. I can't overstate the importance of cultivating your relationships, especially in the media space—the real secret of successful publicity campaigns.

Media relationships should be mutually beneficial. You want the media to publicize your product and service, and the media want you to provide publishable stories. Always keep in mind these four rules:

1. You are a resource for the media.
2. It's never personal.
3. The media can change the rules, but you can't.
4. All that the media think about is what you can do for them and their audience.

Attend networking functions at which you can meet members of the media. Join the local press club. Hang out at the bars, coffee shops and restaurants they frequent. Become a media resource to them. Ask what they're working on. Get their contact info so it's easy to get in touch with them.

Once you've established a media contact, stay in touch with that person, email being the preferred method of contact these days. Play by the media rules. They have the upper hand. They have the power. It's very important that you stay on their radar screen. Remember this and you'll become a public relations superstar!

Websites and List Building

If you've decided to market online, the first rule of which you should be aware is the rule of '*thirds*'. You should determine the budget you'll have for online marketing, then invest one-third in developing your site, one-third in promoting your site and one-third in maintaining your site. Most ill-advised online marketers invest three-thirds in developing their site, then wonder why they aren't earning landmark profits.

Guerrillas know that no matter how brilliant their site, it's invisible and powerless unless people know it's there. That's why the moment they think of going online, they think of how they'll promote their online *and* offline presence. Previously, their advertising had to sell a product or a service. Now, all it has to do is get people to visit their website.

I could write a whole book on Internet marketing but, in a nutshell, here is the three-step process on Internet marketing.

1. Begin with a wonderful product or service.
2. Create a motivational website.
3. Promote or send emails (to your list) with hyperlinks to your website.

This brings me on to the topic of *list building* which is a process of defining your market, setting your objectives and then figuring how to establish warm and trusting relationships with the people on your list.

Firstly, make sure you get permission from people to be on your mailing list. The term for this process is called '*opt in*'. Let your prospects decide whether they want to be on your list. If they opt out, that's cool because you won't have to waste time, money or hopes on them. If they opt in, they want to hear from you and they'll anticipate each contact from you. People who opt in (you may be reading this book because you opted in to one of my lists) will never consider your email to be spam.

Secondly, you can get some of those names by offering a free newsletter, free report or free e-book on your site. The idea is to offer valuable free information—especially unique data that is not available elsewhere—and keep a list of people who sign up or order your freebie. Contests, sweepstakes, free e-zines and joint ventures are more obvious ways to add names to your list. You'll attract many more with your blog and your participation in forums and groups, especially on social media sites. You'll begin with a few names at first. Keep it up and you'll get 5,000, 10,000, 50,000. People aren't changing that fast. They still love valuable free information.

I'm going to share something with you that I normally only share with my high-level students and clients on my JV Programs. The *best* list you can build is a list where people have actually paid to be on it. So how do you give away free information and still get people to pay for it? Simple, you create a CD or DVD that can be shipped to the prospect and charge them for *'shipping and handling'*. In this way, the prospect gets something of immense value, i.e. your *free* training dvd or *free* interview dvd and you build a list of people who have spent some money and will most likely spend more with you in the future, rather than freebie hunters. For a really great example of my best converting web site that does exactly this go to ***www.MillionDollarPartnering.com.***

Social Media

Let's just look at some latest statistics: There are over 1 billion users on Facebook, 750 tweets a second are delivered through Twitter, LinkedIn has over 200 million members and 1 million groups and the Google +1 button is used over 5 billion times a day. So this must tell you that you need to not only be up-to-speed on how to use these platforms but also be using them on a regular basis. Social media has made it easy for anyone without a marketing budget to get results similar to those of corporate companies spending millions. One of the best ways to use this platform is to follow the 4 rules of successful guerrilla social media marketing.

1. Create a response.
2. Engage.
3. Reach out.
4. Share.

Create a Response

Whenever I post on Facebook, Twitter, LinkedIn, Google+, etc, my intention is to create a response or as they say in marketing, a *direct response,* from people reading my posts to get them to do something, whether it's answering a question or visiting one of my websites to download a free report or claim a free dvd. I even get people to 'Like' my posts to gauge who is actually reading them.

Engage

The biggest secret to social media is *engagement*—this is the key to becoming successful and influencing people. Engaging other people into a dialogue and making them take action is the mechanism of a successful social media marketing strategy. Also, the more people you engage with the bigger your following becomes and the more well-known you become in the process.

Reach Out

I'm going to share with you how I can connect with almost anybody using social media and I just hope that none of my celebrity, millionaire or billionaire friends actually read this part! I cover more about how to connect authentically with people in a later chapter. However, for the sake of you, the reader, I will cover one of my all-time favourite strategies for reaching out to people.

Say, for example, you want to reach out on Facebook to someone famous. Most of the time famous people will have a book which you don't need to own, just go to Amazon and look up the book to scan the first few chapters for free. Then take out a line or two of a paragraph on a particular page and message the person saying, 'I absolutely loved your book [name] especially page 6 where you mentioned [sentence]. I just wanted to reach out and say thank you for inspiring me!'

Once you have sent out the message, do nothing, just sit back and wait for a reply. Most of the time you will receive a reply directly from the person saying thank you. When you receive a reply, now you can engage them in a dialogue and send them something of value that will help them. For example, I send people a copy of my $500 joint venture manual that is used by students on my $15,000 and $25,000 programs and say, 'I just wanted to send you something that I believe will really help you in your business'. Then again do nothing, just sit back and wait for a reply.

Now, once they reply they may say, 'Thank you so much, that was great, is there anything can I do for you?'—once you get a reply like that, just ask them for 5-10 minutes of their time for a short phone call so you can not only engage them further but also learn from them. I have used this strategy many times and have ended up becoming friends with some very well-known people who also invite me over for tea, etc, whenever I'm travelling to their country to speak or train.

Share

This one thing has made social media famous and many start-up entrepreneurs who create businesses that allow people to share using social media very rich. Sharing is the epitome of social media and is what people love doing. It also means that now you can share your thoughts and business with the world and, if it goes viral, you may hit the jackpot. Just look at how many views the famous Gangnam Style video received from sharing—over 1 billion!

Webinars

Basically, a webinar is a seminar conducted over the Internet. A webinar can be live or pre-recorded (which is being used a lot recently) with information conveyed according to an agenda, with starting and ending times. In most cases, the presenter speaks over a standard telephone line or through a computer, using Internet telephony to point out information being presented on screen using a Powerpoint presentation, and an audience that can respond over their own telephones or computer. A webcam is sometimes used so the audience can see the presenter.

Most people use webinars to sell a product or for training purposes. I have used webinars for coaching and selling products via joint ventures. Guerrillas like webinars for a variety of reasons.

- There's no travel or out-of-office time; simply attend wherever you have a computer, Internet access and a telephone.
- You can present to a few people—or a few thousand. I've conducted webinars for just 8 people and for 1,000 people.

- Webinars allow you to deliver a well-structured online presentation with Web-enabled text and visuals, along with voice.

Many successful businesses also use webinars to hold virtual company meetings, train clients, students and suppliers geographically and generate sales leads. Right now, Google is also competing in the space with their *hangouts* which let people conduct free webinar-style hangouts online.

Speaking

This one strategy has made me so much money in such a short amount of time that it has to be included in this section. To get started, you can speak at clubs as many organizations in your community would be delighted to have a lunchtime speaker for thirty minutes at no cost. It's cool to give your website at the end of the presentation. I normally give a website address where people can download the presentation for free and I get their contact details for following up.

I know that the greatest fear on earth is the fear of public speaking. However, once you get past that fear the rewards are amazing! Make sure you have a great story and great content as I have found this to be the formula that works! Once you have gained some recognition as a speaker, you can start either charging for your *keynote speech* at conferences and events (I normally charge between $10,000 and $20,000 for mine) or become a platform speaker and sell from the stage—this is something I do more nowadays. My best day ever was in Atlanta when I made $120,000 from a 15 minute presentation on stage *without* pitching!

To get started, contact your local Chamber of Commerce to learn which organizations exist in your community. Keep in mind that they'll relish the thought of having a free speaker delivering fascinating information. This will help you establish yourself as an authority in your field. After that, the world is your oyster!

CHAPTER 3

GUERRILLA MARKETING WEAPONS

A true guerrilla marketing attack begins with your awareness of the 200 weapons; Finally you discover the combination of weapons that produces the most profit for you

— Jay Conrad Levinson

Remember, guerrilla marketing is not about having the biggest budget or the largest marketing department, it's about achieving success using unconventional means. It is not complicated. It is about being creative, patient and strategic. It is about using guerrilla marketing weapons to achieve your goals.

Jay created his first list of guerrilla marketing weapons many years ago and I have updated them. Some of these weapons will work for you, others will not as every business is different. Which of these weapons can you use? You can also check out *www.MillionDollarPartnering.com* for the most current list.

200 Guerrilla Marketing Weapons

1. Your marketing plan(s)
2. A marketing calendar
3. Your Brand Identity
4. Business cards
5. Stationery (digital and print)
6. Personal letters
7. Telephone marketing
8. A toll-free number
9. A vanity phone number
10. The Yellow Pages
11. Postcards
12. Classified ads
13. Free ads in shoppers
14. Per-order and per-inquiry advertising
15. Circulars and flyers
16. Community bulletin boards
17. Magnetic and vinyl car signs
18. Movie ads
19. Outside signs
20. Street banners
21. A window display
22. Inside signs
23. Posters
24. Door-to-door canvassing
25. Door hangers
26. An elevator pitch
27. A value story
28. Upsells and cross-sells
29. Letters of recommendation
30. Attendance at trade shows
31. Direct mail
32. Television commercials
33. Newspaper ads
34. Radio spots
35. Magazine ads
36. Billboards
37. Online directories
38. Craigslist
39. Digital business card
40. Social media accounts
41. Check-in services accounts
42. Mobile phone / smart phone
43. List building (email / direct mail)
44. Personalized email
45. An effective email signature
46. Mobile website
47. Mobile applications (apps)
48. Video email
49. Videos posted to YouTube

50. A domain name/corporate website
51. A geo-niche domain name/ website
52. A landing / squeeze page
53. A merchant account
54. Ecommerce enabled website
55. Auto-responders
56. A good search engine ranking
57. RSS feeds
58. Blogs
59. Podcasting
60. Online Reviews
61. Links from social bookmarking sites
62. e-Books
63. Content creation
64. Webinars
65. Joint ventures
66. Word-of-mouse
67. Viral marketing
68. eBay and other auction sites
69. Click analyzers
70. Pay per-click ads
71. Money keywords
72. Google Adwords
73. Sponsored links
74. Reciprocal link exchanges
75. Banner exchanges
76. Website conversion rates
77. Electronic brochures
78. Google+ Local pages
79. Specific customer data
80. Case studies
81. Sharing
82. Brochures
83. Catalogs
84. Research studies / white papers
85. Public service announcements
86. A newsletter
87. Speeches
88. Free consultations
89. Free demonstrations
90. Free seminars
91. Articles
92. Columns
93. Writing books
94. Publishing-on-demand
95. Workshops
96. Tele-seminars
97. Infomercials
98. Constant learning
99. Marketing insight
100. Yourself
101. Your employees and reps
102. A designated guerrilla
103. Employee attire
104. Your social demeanor
105. Your target audience

106. Your circle of influence
107. Your "Hellos" and "Goodbyes"
108. Your listening skills
109. Your teaching ability
110. Your community-building ability
111. Sales training
112. Stories
113. Networking
114. Professional titles
115. Affiliate marketing
116. Media contacts
117. "A"-List customers
118. Your core story
119. A sense of urgency, scarcity
120. Limited time or quantity offers
121. A call-to-action
122. Satisfied customers
123. A benefits list
124. Competitive advantages
125. Exceptional customer experiences
126. Multi-channel marketing
127. Public relations
128. Fusion marketing
129. Barter/contra
130. Word-of-mouth
131. Buzz
132. Community involvement
133. Club and association memberships
134. Promotional products / swag
135. A tradeshow booth
136. Special events
137. Memorable name tag
138. uxury box at events
139. Gift certificates
140. Audio-visual aids
141. Advertising
142. Reprints and blow-ups of mag ads
143. Coupons
144. A free trial offer
145. Guarantees
146. Contests and sweepstakes
147. Baking or crafts ability (for gifting)
148. Lead buying
149. Follow-up
150. A tracking plan
151. Marketing-on-hold
152. Branded entertainment
153. Product placement
154. Being a radio talk show guest
155. Being a TV talk show guest
156. Crowd-sourcing
157. A proper view of marketing
158. Brand name awareness
159. Intelligent positioning

160. Knowledge of your market
161. A meme
162. A theme line
163. Writing ability
164. Copywriting ability
165. Headline copy talent
166. Location
167. Hours of operation
168. Days of operation
169. Credit card acceptance
170. Financing availability
171. Credibility
172. Reputation
173. Efficiency
174. Quality
175. Service
176. Selection
177. Price
178. Upgrade opportunities
179. Referral program
180. Spying
181. Testimonials
182. Extra value
183. Adopting a noble cause
184. Easy to do business with
185. Honest interest in people
186. Good telephone demeanor
187. Passion and enthusiasm
188. Sensitivity
189. Patience
190. Flexibility
191. Generosity
192. Self-confidence
193. Neatness
194. Aggressiveness
195. Competitiveness
196. High energy
197. Speed
198. Focus
199. Attention to details
200. Ability to take action

PART TWO

MY GUERRILLA STORY

CHAPTER 4

HOW IT ALL STARTED

Out of difficulties grow miracles.

— **Jean De La Bruyere**

 hat I'm about to share with you is my personal journey and the fundamental difference thinking like a true guerrilla can make and spotting the many opportunities in the world today to do joint ventures.

It all began as I was standing in the lobby of one of the top accountancy firms in London, I had made it! Studying hard at University in London and listening to my parents' vision of what I should do with my life and become was a big influence. However, there was something missing; I didn't feel a major accomplishment, I felt there was so much more out there for me and that I had a purpose I needed to fulfil.

It was in the first 6 months of working at the 'corporate establishment' that I finally realised my real passion was helping and connecting people.

I would show people how to use technology more effectively and was also the person that could make the right introductions! It wasn't until my Manager pointed out to me, "Sohail, you seem really passionate about helping and connecting people, you are a real 'people person' and I think you should follow your passion!"

So, the decision was made to leave a high-paying corporate job to follow my passion. I enrolled for an International Masters degree to pursue a career as an IT Consultant and began my journey which would take me on a 'rollercoaster' ride.

It was 1998 and the Internet was in its infancy and people wondered whether this was just a fad or a serious business tool? This really interested me so I started researching what this Internet thing was all about?

I had to write a thesis for my Masters and ended up with the hypothesis, 'The Impact Of The Internet On The Manufacturing Industry'—was this new fad the end of manufacturing industries as we know them and how could businesses utilize the benefits?

I handed the thesis to my Professor with a BIG smile on my face thinking this was a piece of art in 'academic' terms. Little did I know that my Professor liked the thesis so much he actually posted it online through bulletin boards which were the most popular sites back then (Google was officially launched in 1998).

If You Build It They Will Come

Just before I graduated, I started receiving phone calls and emails from venture capital firms and very large 'well known' companies asking me if I could attend a meeting to discuss my research findings on how the Internet could be utilized as a business tool.

So there I was, just before graduating with my Masters, being asked to sit in meetings with the board of directors and venture capitalists; it was truly exciting.

I decided to create a basic e-commerce website selling computer training courses (Powerpoint training slides) on how to use computer applications like word processing, spreadsheets, etc and sell them as downloadable zipped files directly online, as a showcase when I visited prospective clients.

Now back in 1999 it was very EASY to get on the first page of Google and stay there! I was getting lots of traffic and online orders regularly without even doing any advertising to my small e-commerce training site. One of my very first consulting clients was QVC.com and another client which is now one of the top gadget websites in the UK. I picked up a handful of funded .com companies and was being paid between $15,000 and $30,000 per client for online consulting—LIFE WAS GREAT!

The Dot Come Bubble and New Opportunities

It was now 2000 and the inevitable happened—the Dot Com bubble burst! I lost over 80% of my funded clients and had to now figure out what I was going to do to make money as after the bubble and the Y2k bug, being an 'IT Consultant' wasn't a good idea.

I immediately got in touch with a friend of mine who also studied on the same Masters course and was working behind the desk in an unemployment centre. I showed him my small e-commerce training website and told him that it was ticking over making $7,000 a month without any advertising.

We decided to concentrate our efforts on growing this small website and gain more knowledge on how to effectively increase sales.

Two 'Jays' Who Changed My Life

I still remember the day when my eyes opened up to the amazing possibilities of growing your business without growing your marketing spend. My very first two books on 'out of the box' marketing were the original 'Guerrilla Marketing' by Jay Conrad Levinson and another called 'Getting Everything You Can, Out Of All You've Got' by Jay

Abraham whom I now consider both to be the mentors who changed my life.

In both books I read about the concept of 'Joint Ventures and Strategic Alliances' and how anyone can leverage other business's resources and assets for virtually no money down and get them to grow their business exponentially for FREE!

I was hooked, the concept of joint ventures really appealed to me and I set off to find my first joint venture deal to help us grow the business exponentially.

David Approaches Goliath

This was the aftermath of the dot com bubble and Y2k and, just as it is right now, the economy was in a downturn and companies were suffering, especially in the tech sector. We were relatively unknown in the marketplace but we had something that I believed could help companies develop a new profitable revenue stream by leveraging their existing asset—their customer database!

Armed with my instructions from Jay Abraham I approached the biggest IT recruitment company in Europe with a joint venture proposal. I told them that I knew they were suffering in the current economy and that I could help them create an easy and profitable revenue stream using an existing asset that would initially cost them nothing.

They invited me to their posh London offices in Regent Street where 5 people questioned me about this joint venture strategy. Basically, I told them that we had a great converting website that had a suite of popular downloadable computer training products that their database of over 150,000 IT Professionals could purchase and we would give them a percentage for every course sold.

What clinched the deal was that we would handle ALL orders, fulfilment and customer service; all they had to do was send out a regular banner to their database to offer the courses on sale. In our first year our small computer training website did about $85,000. However, in our second year with this one joint venture our turnover jumped from $85,000 to $410,800! So I thought to myself, "This is amazing -how else can we use the power of joint ventures and leverage"?

How To Grow Your Business To 7 Figures Using Licensing

What I'm about to share with you is something called 'licensing'—this is absolutely HUGE! In 2002, the computer training industry was getting savvier and e-learning was growing with not just more high studio quality videos but also a robust learning management system (LMS) for companies to track the users' progress.

We contacted a few companies to obtain quotes for creating high quality e-learning courses and a robust LMS. The costs were ridiculous and we couldn't afford to invest or take a gamble that big. So, we became a reseller of various companies' training products and were now a glorified online storefront promoting other companies' brands instead of our own.

Frustrated by this, I approached a company in the US who had already produced a whole range of very high quality computer training video titles with an advanced LMS which was actually being used by the US government and Fortune 500 companies. I proposed to them that I would like to license their courses to be sold in the UK exclusively through our company and white labelled (branded with our own company name and logos).

After serious negotiations with the CEO (who was one of the most marketing savvy female CEOs I had ever met) we settled on a minimum monthly order commitment of just $10,000 (which was much, much less than us actually producing the material ourselves). That year our business did 7 figures and the investment for taking us to that level was only $10,000!

Now here is the BONUS—I did a deal to purchase courses at 75% below the actual RRP (recommended retail price) which was in dollars! As a matter of fact, they sold their high-end certified computer training course packages in the US for $3,997; we took the same material and just re-branded it and sold it in the UK for £3,997! Yes, through licensing, we were making more per sale than the actual creators of the materials!

You can also use this strategy to your advantage if you own material that you have sold in the past but are not selling anymore. More recently my good friend and well-known marketer, Yanik Silver at *YanikSilver. com*, revealed one of the secrets of his success through licensing his own material to different countries (new markets) and making pure profit while someone else was doing ALL the hard work!

In 2005 I received a brochure through my door from a company called Independent Correspondence Schools (ICS), the largest home study school in the world with over 13 million customers and, while reading their brochure, I noticed they sold home study computer training packages.

I immediately ordered one of their home study computer training courses and was shocked to receive a printed manual and a CD with Powerpoint slides (this rings a bell). I contacted them straight away with a Joint Venture proposal and sent them a copy of a CD based version of one of our video training courses. They loved it and invited me to meet up with their Head of Product Development based in Glasgow.

I told them that we had the exclusive (this is very important) license for the UK and Europe and could re-license and white-label the product for them to sell and distribute in the UK and Europe. We ended up flipping the existing license deal we had and got them to commit to a minimum monthly order commitment of $30,000 with the US company handling ALL the duplication, labelling and shipping while we just took the initial orders and split the profit 50/50 with them.

Always Have an Exit Strategy

It was now 2006 and I was getting quite good at locating lucrative joint venture partners and deals. I was reading the Financial Times Technology Fast Track Report—a rundown on the fastest growing tech companies in the UK—and my eye caught a listing of an online IT hardware and software distribution company that had over 500,000 customers and was then valued at $160 million.

So, naturally the joint venture business expert in me saw an opportunity to get them to promote our computer training courses to their 500,000 customers! It was actually a chance meeting at a charitable event when I met the Chairman of the group who was heavily involved in charity work. I introduced myself and, after chatting for a while he said, "Sohail, I really like you and what you're doing, drop by my office for a chat".

Armed with my joint venture proposal and pitch I showed up at a very prestigious glass building ready to do a deal. I was waiting in the lobby and was immediately asked to make my way up to the top floor to the Chairman's office. Once inside the office, I sat down opposite the Chairman and his son who was the MD. They turned to me and said, "Sohail, thanks for coming, we have decided that we really do not want to do a joint venture with you". I stood up and was ready to leave when they added, "Actually, Sohail, we are really interested in buying your business!"

My jaw dropped. At that time I had 2 partners and was not in a position to make a decision and didn't even had an exit strategy ready!

We had a brief discussion about why they thought what we offered would integrate nicely into one of their IT business services divisions. They were making acquisitions due to having a strong balance sheet and had to start making some investments. So, with a HUGE smile on my face, I left their offices without making any firm decisions and went to tell the good news to my business partners.

Creating An 8-Figure Business Using Joint Ventures

I can remember that day very clearly. It was late 2006 and we finally decided to sell a majority stake in the business to the large IT group in a part cash/part equity deal because we believed that they didn't know the business as well as we did. The business was now worth multi-millions and within 12 months of leveraging their 500,000 customer database we had managed to double the business again!

Life was great. After building the business using joint ventures and then eventually selling to the IT group, I was living in the house of my dreams, a Georgian mansion, had a red Ferrari, Porsche and BMW on the drive and a successful business with over 20 staff and some great clients. What could go wrong?

From 8-Figures To Zero

This is a day that I will never forget. It was a negative point in my life which actually turned into a blessing. It was early 2008 and the recession had caught out a lot of people including very well-known high street retailers, there were casualties everywhere.

Sales dropped slightly and we compensated by offering a lower price package to those people who had less money to spend than before. Unknown to me, the group company that owned a majority stake in my business and was the power behind the marketing, was in trouble.

The signs started appearing when we would not be involved in meetings with the heads of the group and started seeing them layoff people due to downsizing. One thing led to another and the group company made a decision to go into administration informing us about it a few days later.

The end result was that without the support from the group company and with further complications, I ended up losing the business, my luxury home and the red Ferrari.

Time To Reflect

So what do you do when you LOSE everything you've worked the last 8 years of your life for? You seek solace and support in loved ones! My support network has always been my family.

I moved back home to my parents' house where my spare room was still available. Hot meals and a decent roof over my head gave me time to reflect upon where I went from here.

Naturally, I was upset and worried about my future. You read stories of entrepreneurs losing their millions only to come back bigger and better. Is this what I really wanted?

Don't get me wrong, I have always had a very strong mindset and entreprencurial spirit, but I wasn't that young get-up-and-go-kid anymore. Also, did I want to re-build my lost empire, including all the headaches it brought?

It was time to do some soul searching. I packed my bags and decided to go traveling for a few months to visit spiritual places and find my direction in life. I was 3 weeks' into my spiritual journey when I realised that' *once an entrepreneur, always an entrepreneur*' and I would seek my next business challenge, no matter what.

By now it was 2009 and I decided to return home and start plotting my future success map. One thing I identified that has always stuck with me.is the saying, 'Jack of All Trades, Master of None' I spent a few months trying all sorts of business ideas and opportunities, becoming frustrated along the way.

I asked myself: "How can I get myself back up to where I used to be, as quickly as possible without a budget, product or existing customers and what one thing am I really good at that has actually worked?" Then it hit me—joint ventures!

CHAPTER 5

ZERO TO 4 MILLION CUSTOMERS IN 30 DAYS

To succeed… you need to find something to hold on to, something to motivate you, something to inspire you.

— Tony Dorsett

I had nothing to lose if I just went out and focused on the BIG deals to make the maximum amount of money in a short space of time. If it didn't work out, I would still be in the same position that I was in already, right?

I sat down, took pen to paper and wrote my goal for the year, 'To Make One Million Dollars In The Next 12 Months'!

Now all I had to do was find some BIG lucrative joint venture deals and I was on my way. Let me tell you, when you are adept at doing high-level joint ventures like me, you see opportunities everywhere, whether its under-utilized assets in the form of advertising space on office buildings or first floor windows, to re-activating gym memberships for a chain of gym clubs by creating a 'welcome back' book of gift vouchers donated from complementary businesses.

The Millionaire Mindset

If you have ever been to one of the many seminars that teach people how to develop a 'millionaire mindset', let me tell you that most people attending will never become millionaires.

Don't get me wrong, I have met and followed the teachings of many success gurus like T Harv Eker and Tony Robbins very closely. However, knowledge without action is just that, its knowledge.

You see, people create barriers of self-belief that stop them from becoming millionaires. Now you may be saying, "Sure Sohail, you have actually been a multi-millionaire so it's easy for you to become one again!" I would have to disagree with that because what has made me successful is not the money in the bank, it's the persistence coupled with action to become successful.

How many of you have actually sat in your dream car or walked in to view a million dollar house just to be able to visualize and feel what success has waiting for you? You must eat, drink and sleep success because it will eventually come knocking on your door!

I'm a big believer in the Law of Attraction and putting out signals to the universe to bring me those opportunities or show me the direction. Now without action you will not get any results so please don't sit there at home just visualizing, expecting success to come to you.

The best tool I can recommend is creating a 'vision board' with all the things you want to achieve. This has helped me tremendously.

Tough Economies Create Better Opportunities

Recessions are a godsend for joint venture experts like me! Remember I told you the story of my first joint venture deal and how I approached and closed one of the biggest recruitment companies for a joint venture because they were suffering in the economic downturn?

Well guess what, during a recession, companies begin looking for alternative revenue streams to replace their existing declining ones.

Look around you and see which companies that would never have originally entered into a partnership with you are now willing to look at proposals.

Spotting The Opportunity Of a Lifetime

The biggest joint venture deal that I have ever done to date came by chance. I was reading a copy of a national newspaper on a Sunday (like I normally do, full of great direct-response ads!) and came across a one-page full ad for a book called, 'How To Use Your PC In Just 2 Hours'. What really interested me was reading that they had sold over 400,000 copies of this small book which got my joint venture mind thinking.

My good friend and online marketing guru, Mike Filsaime at *MikeFilsaime.com*, calls this 'hyper awareness'. When I was in New York visiting him, we had a conversation about how some people have 360 degree radar and can spot opportunities at every angle; most visionary entrepreneurs and JV experts have this amazing ability.

I ordered a copy of the book to have a look at it and also did some more research into the company which turned out to be a very large direct mail and catalogue company for the 'silver surfer or baby boomer' market.

The Cheeky Business Proposal

Having received the book, I was excited to see the opportunities that this company was missing and contacted them with my proposal. I told them that I had purchased the book and asked whether they have a video training version of the book? They replied that they didn't and I countered by saying that I had a video training course (which I actually didn't at the time) that I thought they could sell to their existing customers who had purchased the original book.

Again, they asked me to submit a proposal to the Marketing Manager and I received an email from the Managing Director inviting me in to a meeting to discuss the proposal further. Without giving away too much this was a very savvy company with an 8-figure turnover and only three employees—the Managing Director, the Financial Director and the Marketing Manager. Everything else was outsourced.

At the meeting, after discussing the joint venture proposal, I was asked to produce a copy of the video training course for them to evaluate. I had to make an excuse to cover myself and was told to get a copy over to them in the next 7 days. I left the meeting knowing that they wanted to do a deal but needed to see the actual product first.

The Beauty Of Outsourcing

Having no actual product to show them, I began trying to source the product from local manufacturers. I contacted a few and mentioned that I had clients that could sell a few thousand units of their video based training course and we just needed to be able to negotiate on the buying and selling price. Nearly ALL the companies I contacted didn't understand the power of joint ventures and were stuck in their 'one-size-fits-all' mindset of a standard reseller discount which is the norm in their industry.

Having just 5 days left to produce a viable product for evaluation, I decided to shift from the manufacturers to outsourcing using www.elance.com, a website where freelancers bid for the projects you post. Hopeful this was the way forward, I posted a 5-day project for a video training course to be developed, based on the contents of the original computer book and people started bidding on the project. By day 5, I had a high-quality, tailored product created which cost me just $500 and for which I owned the rights. The title of the computer book was

'How To Master Your Computer In Just Two Hours', the video version was titled, 'How To Master Your Computer In Just One Hour'.

The 7 Figure Joint Venture

Armed with a copy of the video course on DVD, I went to see the direct mail company for them to evaluate it. They loved it! Little did they know that it was a basic Camtasia (screen recording software) video course that was very easy to create. Straight away they asked the question, "Sohail, what other titles have you got?"

I had to convince them that it was in their best interest to promote the video course to their existing 400,000 customers first before we even considered creating more titles. Once we were on the same page, I began probing the Managing Director for some solid statistics, asking him how many people who had previously purchased the computer book would possibly purchase the video version.

Now this company knew their statistics very well and the Managing Director mentioned that within the next 12-18 months at least 50% of the current customer base would upgrade to the video version of the computer book. OK, we now have a potential 200,000 units and just needed to lock down the percentage that I would put in my pocket. If you have ever heard of a company called QVC, then you would know that they operate on a royalty basis where they pay you a small percentage (normally 5-10%) of achieved sales; this is the standard in the direct mail/catalogue industry.

My normal commission (which sometimes involves an upfront retainer) on joint venture deals is between 20% and 50%. In order to accept a smaller commission/royalty, I proposed a licensing arrangement where the company would do ALL the duplication, packaging and fulfilment and I would grant them a license to duplicate the product for an agreed commission to me of just $7.50 per unit sold. So, let's recap: 200,000 units at $7.50 per unit sold is $1,500,000 for this joint venture deal. It actually took us close to 17 months to complete this deal and we did just over 201,462 units.

An Astonishing Revelation

The Million Dollar Joint Venture was not the icing on the cake. Having prepared the joint venture contract for signing, I presented it to the Managing Director who mentioned that if this product sold well, he would like to roll it out to the rest of his customer database. When I asked, "What do you mean, 'the rest of?'", he replied "Sohail, we have 4.2 million customers"!.

This is how I went 'From Zero To 4 Million Customers In Just 30 Days.' I now assist them as their official Joint Venture Broker to help find complementary products in the health and wellbeing market that can be promoted to their 4.2 million customers.

My Journey With Joint Ventures

These past few years have literally been a rollercoaster for me. I've been invited to speak worldwide on the topic of 'Joint Ventures and Business Growth', train individuals and business owners how to use joint ventures, become involved in more 7-figure joint venture deals/launches AND built amazing relationships with some of the world's top business and marketing experts.

My approach to doing joint ventures is always unorthodox however, for those of you who have a great product or invention and need help with getting it ready for approaching partners such as manufacturers, catalogs, retailers or mail order houses we offer a product partnering service at *www.MillionDollarPartnerning.com*.

CHAPTER 6

JOINT VENTURE BROKERING AND DEAL MAKING

If you help enough people get what they want, you will eventually get what you want.

— **Zig Ziglar**

 make *lots of money* by simply being a middleman. In joint ventures, the middleman is called the "joint venture broker" or 'deal maker'.

As a joint venture broker, you'll:

- look for hidden or under-utilized assets within a company,
- create marketing opportunities that are either unrealised or unrecognised,
- exploit customer lists that are not maximised,
- recognize relationships that can be optimised.

The role of the joint venture broker changes depending upon the nature of the joint venture. The joint venture broker might be a person who finds joint venture partners, or it might be a person who sets up the deal. In both cases, the joint venture broker is compensated for his or her role by taking a percentage of the profits

Joint venture brokering is not a difficult concept to understand. Just imagine an orchestra. Surely, such an ensemble wouldn't be able to play marvellous music without the conductor? The conductor simply brings all the band members together and instructs them how to proceed with a masterpiece. The conductor doesn't have to play any musical instruments; he just needs a good working knowledge of music.

The kind of joint ventures you can arrange are as unlimited as your imagination. A car dealer can offer a free dinner at a local restaurant to anyone who comes in for a test drive. Both the restaurant and the car dealer get more customers to come through their doors and add, potentially to their customer list. The sporting goods store forms a relationship with the health club or gym, each sending the other customers for fitness and equipment purchases. The electricity company agrees to include an ad for an appliance dealer in its next billing letter, reaching every utility user in the region. The electricity company is happy because they reduce their cost of mailing because the appliance dealer pays a small fee for each insert. The appliance dealer is happy because they piggy-back on the electricity company, gain access to all their customers, and with less cost than conducting a mailing from scratch.

Joint venture brokering appeals to many entrepreneurs because it offers a way to earn really good money without having to create your own product, without having to set up and implement any marketing strategies (although for some types of joint ventures, a knowledge of marketing is essential) and, more often than not, without having to invest anything financially.

The joint venture broker essentially determines the type of resources the client needs, and works with the client to determine what can be offered to joint venture partners who have those resources.

The joint venture broker then works out how to present the offer to joint venture partners so that they see the offer as a win-win-win situation. (The three "wins" are a win for the client, a win for the joint venture partner, and a win for the customer as well.)

Approaching potential joint venture partners in just the right way is vital to the outcome of the joint venture. The joint venture broker's role is to assist the client when trying to convince people who have never heard of the client to enter into a joint venture deal through a well-crafted joint venture proposal.

The joint venture broker has already determined what a potential joint venture partner can gain from the deal. Having done their research, they know who needs what resources and how to find others to provide those resources

I've always told people who asked me about joint venture brokering that in order to be a successful joint venture broker a person MUST possess the following requisites:

- A good knowledge of your industry.
- A comprehensive and diverse network of contacts.
- Good communication and negotiating skills.
- A creative mindset.
- A will to succeed.

These requisites, of course, will be covered in the sections to come.

What this book cannot teach you, however, is the will to succeed. This must come from within you. Anyone can try their best to bring out the competitive fire within you, but you alone must be able to conjure that fire and use it to your advantage.

Some of the roles you may be called on to fill as a joint venture broker include:

- Managing the complete joint venture.
- Planning the joint venture.
- Reviewing terms of service for the project.
- Consulting with clients on joint venture partners.
- Day-to-day operation, support and advice on the joint venture.
- Reviewing and assessing products/services from a marketing perspective.
- Locating, analyzing and recruiting top producing joint venture partners.
- Screening, reviewing and approving potential joint venture partners.
- Monitoring and motivating underperforming joint venture partners.
- Maintaining contact with joint venture partners, handling all emails/calls.
- Working with joint venture partners on improving conversions.
- Reporting issues and resolving potential problems.

The Benefits of Being a joint venture broker or deal maker

Joint venture brokering is such a lucrative and exclusive field. Knowing all the advantages you can derive in a career as a joint venture broker will develop within you a love for this job, like I have. Loving your work is, of course, essential to your success.

Joint Venture Brokering, you see, is a highly creative business. It may not seem apparent right now but, trust me, there is more creativity involved in joint venture brokering than in any other field of marketing.

Joint venture brokering, being the highly creative avenue that it is, will require a passion for the business. This is why you should love what you're doing. When you're passionate about your career, it will feel less like work, more like fun, and it will spark your creative genius at the same time!

Let's take a look at the benefits that can be brought about from being a joint venture broker:

- You don't need to spend years building your customer list and constantly trying to build a better relationship with your subscriber base.
- You don't need to keep track of the sales made, of how much money is owed to whom, of fulfilling the product and sending it out, etc.
- You just step in, leverage those resources, and make colossal profits by bringing people together and contributing to others.
- You will be known as an expert that makes things happen and more opportunities will fall in your lap.
- There will always be a need for a joint venture broker as long as businesses seek out fresh ideas to expand their enterprises and increase their profits, and seek out other businesses that compliment theirs, a Joint Venture Broker will always be in demand.
- As a joint venture broker your market is not seasonal in nature. Demand for your services runs for the whole duration of each and every passing year.

Not only is joint venture brokering a great way of earning a fantastic living, it is also a marvellous way of positioning yourself as an established personality in the marketing field.

Imagine… if you're able to broker a gigantic deal that revolutionizes the industry because of its sheer size and the imagination that inspired it, you will forever be known as the mind that authored the project that people talk about for many years—you may even be invited to speak at some very high-profile events worldwide, like I have!

Joint Venture Brokering Commissions and Fees

This is perhaps the question that you wanted to ask from the very beginning: "How exactly do I make money as a joint venture broker?"

As you know by now, by being a joint venture broker, you will be investing your time, efforts, expertise and skills in a project that promises to reap a lot of benefits for the partners you court. The things you contribute to the joint venture should not go unrewarded, right? Joint venture brokering is a business, not a charity, after all.

The first thing you need to do is determine what kind of arrangement you want to employ when it comes to your earnings from the joint venture. We will discuss different types of joint ventures in a later chapter.

Here are your choices:

1. <u>A percentage from each sale</u>. This is a highly lucrative option. The ultimate goal of a joint venture is to boost the number of sales that are enjoyed by the partners. Imagine if you had a share of every successful sale. There would be no limit to how much money you can earn! However, you have to bear in mind that this set up is greatly dependent upon how much success the joint venture achieves.

2. <u>A percentage from the total profit after the period of the joint venture</u>. This will seem more amenable for the partners you are courting. However, your profit margin from this set up may be a little more uncertain.

3. <u>A share as a partner</u>. Joint venture brokers can always bargain to become business partners. Basically, a business partner is one who invests work on the project instead of finances and/or resources. By being a business partner and actively participating

in the actual operation of the joint venture, you can justify receiving a share equivalent to the other partners.

4. <u>A fixed rate</u>. You could impose a fixed rate for your services. This is similar to a standard consultant charging for his services. But you have to make sure that your rate will be proportionate to the profit that can be expected from the joint venture you brokered. This set up is advantageous because the amount you will receive will not be contingent on the success of the project. However, you might end up regretting such a decision if the joint venture proves to be a blockbuster. For example, I charge a fixed $10,000 fee to find and connect targeted high-level strategic partners for $1M+ clients over a 10 week period.

5. <u>A hybrid of #1 (a commission) and #4 (a fixed rate)</u>. You could charge an upfront or monthly fee to get the client to show that he is serious about pursuing the joint venture, and then still collect a 10% to 20% commission from the sales or the profits. An upfront fee of between $1,000 and $5,000 to begin with, depending upon the nature of the deal, would be acceptable. For example, I charge between $5,000 to $10,000 a month (or a discounted upfront fee) and then a % of sales generated to work with $1M+ clients setting up their strategic partnering platform over a period of 6 months.

Note that for some clients, you may have to deduct the upfront fee from the commissions you receive later. What this does, though, is get the client to follow through with the project and pull his weight in terms of the work as you indicate that the upfront fee is non-refundable, even if the client later changes his or her mind about going forward with the joint venture.

Your choice of share/fee set up would, and should, depend on a careful study of the joint venture. If you are certain that the joint venture will meet your expectations, then a percentage system would be the best option (and most profitable for *you*) to take. If you have doubts as to whether or not the joint venture will achieve blockbuster status, then a fixed rate would be the better route to take.

Of course, you'll need to be more than just a joint venture broker to justify a share equal to that of each of the partners, and you'll also have to commit much labor toward the joint venture.

Once you have decided on a payment scheme, you have to inform the partners of it at the earliest possible time. This will avoid the possibility of being undercut; that is, being neglected after they have taken over the joint venture.

To better protect your interests, put your chosen payment scheme in writing and have the partners attest to it to verify that they have read and agreed to the terms you have given.

Bear in mind if you have to find the joint venture partners and have to educate them on the subject of joint ventures, write the sale letter for the deal, look over everything to make sure it all goes smoothly, manage the whole deal, etc, you may be able to get a much higher percentage (like 40% or so).

One other aspect to consider is whether your percentage is based on gross sales or net profits. The two figures can be *vastly* different. Make sure that you consider this! Often times, you can land a deal that you otherwise wouldn't get by taking a higher percentage of the net profits. If you structure the deal right, you can still come out making more money with a higher percentage of the net profits than with a lower percentage on gross sales. The moral is to look at your numbers carefully!

In a recent conversation with my good friend, CEO of As Seen On TV and star of ABC's Shark Tank Kevin Harrington we identified a need for joint venture brokers to assist inventors find strategic partners like manufacturers and distributors to help make their dreams come true. A true win-win-win opportunity.

Make Money Doing Joint Ventures Amongst Your Own Clients

What if there was a way for you to not only help your current clients make money quickly in the current economy but also for you to profit from it without any work on your part?

You see ALL your clients have under-utilized resources that can be leveraged. These resources could include employees, inventory, office space, advertising space, expertise, money, distribution, databases, customers… the list goes on and on.

As a joint venture broker you need to understand your client's business (which you do) and the business owner's real needs (which you already know).

Once you know what they really want, what their customer acquisition costs are and you have a good idea of the potential lifetime value of each of their customers, you are in a very good position to put together deals between your existing clients.

And of course, you just take a cut of the resulting business—EASY!

Most clients have a problem with sales and marketing. The good news is that joint ventures, set up properly, will solve their problem. Once you learn how to do joint venture deals you can give them exactly what they want without risking any of your own time, money or resources.

Let me give you a quick example to show you how you can set up and use joint venture deals between your existing clients:

Let's say you have a client named Bob who is a personal trainer and, as his business relies on new customers, he is struggling to make ends meet.

You decide to help Bob to do something about his lack of clients using your deal making skills. You contact another one of your clients named Bill, who owns a supplement store, and ask Bill if he could refer his customers to Bob and Bob will do likewise with his clients.

Then, all you have to do is help them with their marketing strategy to increase the response/sales and take a cut of the resulting sales as a joint venture broker fee, while they do ALL the work.

Once you have done one project, for how many of your clients can you actually broker deals, taking a cut of the results?

So you see, whether you are a VA, coach, marketing consultant, insurance salesman, commercial real estate broker, business-to-business broker, etc you can make much MORE money setting up joint venture deals between your existing clients!

Of course, there is a lot more to joint ventures than what I've shared here. You have to protect yourself with proper agreements, making sure you follow a 'proven' system so that everyone in every deal clearly understands what is expected so there is no confusion down the road.

For the last few years, I have been training and certifying joint venture brokers or deal makers all over the world, including the US, UK, Europe and the Middle East. At the time of writing this book we have had some amazing success stories, including one joint venture broker closing a $50,000 deal in 60 minutes and another joint venture broker closing two deals worth $3 Million within 6 months of attending one of my programs; not quite 30 days but a great example of sticking to the program and focusing.

For more details on my 'Million Dollar Partnering Certification' program, locating certified joint venture brokers personally trained by me or to watch an interview I did recently with one of my certified joint venture brokers who closed not one but two 7-figure joint venture deals within 6 months of completing one of my programs, go to ***www. MillionDollarPartnering.com.***

As I close this chapter I want to share with you how POWERFUL Joint ventures really are and why now, more than ever, there is such a demand for this skill. I'm sitting here in my hotel room at the Mandarin Oriental in New York City overlooking Central Park, as I prepare for a day of joint venture brokering and training for a client who paid me $30,000 for the day (including ALL my expenses) to train himself and his sales team on how to create joint ventures within their organisation to generate high-value leads!

In the following chapters I will cover how you can also implement some of the strategies in this book to do the same WITHOUT paying me my standard $30,000 daily fee, unless you really need my personal skills (my contact details are at the back of this book) and knowledge of joint ventures.

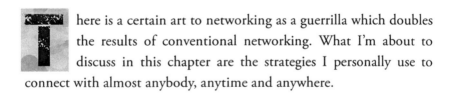

CHAPTER 7

HOW TO NETWORK LIKE A GUERRILLA

What is the most important form of marketing? It is the ability to communicate effectively

— Akio Morita

here is a certain art to networking as a guerrilla which doubles the results of conventional networking. What I'm about to discuss in this chapter are the strategies I personally use to connect with almost anybody, anytime and anywhere.

The Two Most Important Networking Questions

When networking at seminars and events there are only 2 questions you ever need to ask the people with whom you're networking:

1. *How did you get started as a* _____*? (a great ice breaker)*
2. *How can I help you sell more of your* _____*?*

The Top 10 Tips For Networking Success

1. *Make sure you introduce yourself to the Event Organiser and Registration Person.*
2. *Do your homework in advance and pinpoint the people that you want to speak to.*
3. *Keep business cards without cell numbers so you can write them and look personal.*
4. *When receiving a business card, write on it where you met them and the conversation.*
5. *Always use the other person's name two or three times during your conversation.*
6. *Ask the right questions as we covered earlier in the presentation.*
7. *Always network in a high-traffic area like the entrance, the lobby or the bar.*
8. *Introduce each new person you meet to at least another person.*
9. *Book a date in the diary to next contact that person on the day and buy them lunch.*
10. *Follow up within 48 hours by sending your contact a picture and conversation reminder.*

How True Guerrillas Network

To really see how true guerrillas network you need to start attending paid events where you can meet and see some of the true guerrilla marketers in action. For me, it was being invited as a VIP to my good friend Yanik Silver's annual Underground Event in the US, one of the best events for networking that I have ever attended.

How I Connected With Jay Conrad Levinson

I always practice what I preach and before I tell you how I connected with Jay let me go back and explain what I learnt from attending and speaking at many seminars and events around the world.

I mentioned previously how I was invited as a VIP to my good friend Yanik Silver's annual Underground Event. This is where I learnt at first-hand how connectors and super networkers really work. I put up a post on Social Media mentioning that I would be at the event to help find joint venture partners for attendees for free, as a thank you for being invited as a VIP. When I arrived at the event, I was swamped by people showing me their products and asking if I could help.

Now, while I had a bunch of people lining up on my right hand side I felt a hand tap me on my left shoulder. It was a guy who introduced himself as the Affiliate Manager for Ryan Deiss (a very well-known marketing genius) and he asked me if it was OK for him to have a few minutes of my time at dinner which he would pay for, as he knew how busy I was. I agreed and he walked away saying that he would meet me in the restaurant downstairs in the evening. I glanced back at the line of people on my right hand side and started talking to them again. A few minutes later, I had another tap on my shoulder and a guy introduced himself as the Joint Venture Manager for Nitro Marketing which is run by a good friend of mine and multi-millionaire, Kevin Wilke (great guy). Like the person before him, he also asked me to lunch, which he would pay for, so he could have a few minutes of my time as he knew how busy I was. Again, I agreed and he walked away saying that he would meet me in the restaurant downstairs for lunch.

So, what did I learn from this? I learnt that to get people's attention, especially busy and important people, you need to offer them something and when you do they will feel obliged to return the favour. This is known as the '*Law of Reciprocity*' coined by a very interesting guy whom I have had the privilege of meeting, Robert Cialdini, who wrote a book called '*The Psychology of Influence*'. This is a must read for anyone looking to become a super connector!

Back to how I connected with Jay. I was invited to a cruise with some of my fellow members of the $25k Mastermind and was told that Jay Conrad Levinson was the keynote guest speaker. I really wanted to meet Jay and hear his very cool stories (if you knew Jay well, you will know what I mean) and knew that it would be difficult as I was not the only one.

Jay was swamped with people who wanted to take pictures with him and meet him which made it very difficult to get his attention. However, I waited for the right moment and caught him sitting alone in the ship's lobby. I then asked him if it was OK for us to get together for dinner as I knew how busy he was and he agreed. As I walked away, I thought will he even remember? That evening as I walked past his table, where only his family were permitted to sit, Jay called me over and we sat together and told our cool stories to each other over dinner. This led to me sending over a copy of my idea for this book and closing a joint venture deal with Jay to get 'Guerrilla Marketing and Joint Ventures' published for the world to read.

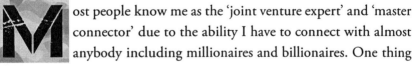

CHAPTER 8

HOW TO CONNECT WITH MILLIONAIRES AND BILLIONAIRES

If you can be interested in other people, you can rule the world
— **Jay Abraham**

ost people know me as the 'joint venture expert' and 'master connector' due to the ability I have to connect with almost anybody including millionaires and billionaires. One thing I have learnt from making millions, losing millions and making my way back to the top very quickly is that it is ALL about the people you surround yourself with and that has been the secret of my success.

There is a famous quote by someone I have personally had the pleasure of meeting and spending time with and that is Robert Kiyosaki. Robert mentions that 'The close people in your network determine your net worth'. Your network is simply a community that you are in, this community has rules, values and beliefs of its own that eventually become your values and beliefs. Remember this: Millionaires network with other millionaires.

Here's a test for you to identify if you are in the right network. Identify the topics of your conversations when you are in your community; do you talk about creating wealth, becoming more successful or simply the weather?

Most times these millionaires are the core influencers in any given industry because of their wealth and financial business success. If you want to become the best in your business field, you must take the initiative of learning how to connect with the core influencers and cultivate their endorsements. Encourage them to respond to your offering in a positive way by connecting using some of my own techniques mentioned in this book. (I normally charge between $15,000 and $25,000 to teach this on my high-level programs). By doing so, you too can become a success in a small fraction of the time it might otherwise take.

Research has shown that millionaires turn networks into cheque books—they leverage who and what they already know to get information, introductions, advice and financial, emotional and practical support. This is something I do all the time within my own high-level network.

The secret is to actively listen to the needs of the other person which is easier said than done. For example, don't be afraid to offer help by asking questions such as 'How can I be helpful?' or 'Would it be helpful if I...' Maybe they need an introduction to a firm or a person—I call this 'connecting the dots'—and, if you do that, you become more relevant to that person and they'll be there for you too. So, don't focus on what you can get, focus on what you can give.

In the past, it was much harder to connect with millionaires and billionaires. However, today there is no reason why you can't reach people you don't know, thanks to the online Social Media tools like Facebook, Twitter and LinkedIn. Social Media is now used by everyone and it has therefore become easier to reach out and communicate with people you would have never been able to connect with before.

Those people who really know me will tell you that I'm a 'Social Media Ninja' and use it to find and connect with core influencers. I use a different tactic and regularly commend them on something that they have done recently or I mention a paragraph from their book that I may be reading. What eventually happens is that they usually get back to me with a thank you and this is when the dialogue begins as I slowly bring them on to having a short phone call with me so I can ask about the projects that they are currently working on and how I can support them. My whole ethos is centered around 'Give first, ask later' and guess what?—it works!

High level connectors like me gain endorsements for reasons that go beyond the basic products or services we offer. We do extraordinary things, that's the difference. For example, I always aim to enhance the profit/sales of whoever I'm connecting with first. In other words, I always open with the question, "How can I help you sell more of your product or service?" I always give this help before asking for anything and, in return, the millionaire will then go out of his way to endorse me to his network.

Most millionaires and billionaires that I know are members of one or more affinity groups. These groups include professional societies, philanthropic associations, political groups, alumni associations and even masterminds (as mentioned continuously in Napoleon Hill's classic, Think and Grow Rich).

Recently I was at a billionaire's 40,000 square foot mansion in Tampa attending one of the $25k Mastermind Groups that I belong to which is run by a close friend of Tony Robbins, the motivational guru. Let me tell you something; when I first joined this group I felt like I had been catapulted to an entirely new level of thinking and business! Why? Because I was surrounded by incredibly bright, talented, successful and generous millionaires and billionaires who were just as interested in my success as I was in theirs.

To connect with millionaires and billionaires you must provide something of value to them. Don't forget these are extremely busy people and do not have time for idle chat. Personally, I believe that everybody has something to offer and the important need here is a solution to remove their pain or problem. If you dedicate yourself to serve others, then you will make that connection happen.

A recent example of this was when I offered my joint venture networking skills for free to a millionaire event promoter in the US where I would spend 15 minutes warming up the audience with a really cool joint venture exercise. The last time I did this in Atlanta, I made $120,000 without pitching any of my programs—not bad for 15 minutes' work. One of the reasons I did this was to meet with some of the speakers and also be on the same stage as them so I could build my connections.

The result was even more incredible than I could have imagined as I not only made some high-level connections but also got to speak on stage for a full hour, met my current publisher at the event who offered me a book deal after watching me speak and was also invited by another promoter to speak at an event alongside one of my peers, now good friend, super motivational speaker AND twice #1 New York Times bestselling author Brendon Burchard.

The good thing about doing joint ventures is that it is a great win for everybody involved and that is what really adds value. At the time of writing this book, I have secured access to the billionaire's 40,000 square foot mansion in the US for my own 'Million Dollar Partnering Intensives' and 'Million Dollar Partnering Mastermind,' without paying to use the facility. Instead, a percentage of the profit will be split between the owner and myself. This is a strategy I have used again and again. Another millionaire client of mine owns a few luxury villas in Spain and one of them, which can accommodate up to 10 people, with a private pool, stays empty for most of the year. If you have an asset like this that can be leveraged in any way, please contact me. For more details on my 'Million Dollar Partnering Intensives' and 'Million Dollar Partnering Mastermind' go to *www.MillionDollarPartnering.com*.

The lesson learnt is to always be interesting and have a really cool story (like I do) that you can share and encourage them to connect with you. Give as much value as you can, putting yourself in that person's shoes when asking how you can help them. I have personally made so many high-level connections because of this strategy and also offer this as a service to others who need to make connections (for a fee of course).

One of my good friends and fellow connector to millionaires and billionaires, Larry Benet, says that *'You will always attract the people you think about'*. The Law of Attraction really does work if you think about attracting prosperity and millionaires into your life AND take action towards those things, thereby increasing the chance of it happening.

I invite you to think about the people you are networking with and are surrounded by. Are they in the same place you want to go? Or, are they where you currently are? Do they support you dreams and ambitions? Or, are they secretly threatened by your success? You will be surprised by the answers, which will help you gain more focus and clarity towards success. Keep me updated on your progress.

PART THREE

MILLION DOLLAR PARTNERING

CHAPTER 9

MILLION DOLLAR PARTNERING USING JOINT VENTURES

The ability to leverage what you don't own AND profit from it is pure business magic

— **Sohail Khan**

A joint venture (also known as a JV or strategic alliance) is an arrangement that will be of mutual benefit between two (or more) people, businesses or companies who have complementary resources or assets that can be leveraged.

What do I mean by resources or assets? I mean products, services, machinery, equipment, buildings, unused capacity and a customer list (or mailing list) that can be leveraged by the owner or whoever approaches the owner with a joint venture proposal (covered in a later chapter).

Joint ventures are known under many names. Some refer to them as "tie-ins", "collaborative marketing", "strategic alliances", "endorsement marketing", "hidden asset marketing", "reciprocal marketing" or, as Jay Conrad Levinson calls them, "fusion marketing". Regardless, all these terms essentially refer to the same thing and, if you just look around, you'll see many examples there in the world. For example, when you see a commercial for McDonald's you almost see a pitch for Coca-Cola.

The idea of the joint venture is as simple as: Business A agrees to include Business B's brochure or an endorsed letter in their next mailing, either for a fee, a percentage, or if Business B agrees to do the same for them. The result is instant access to a whole new influx of customers without having to spend any money on advertising or market research to find them.

A joint venture is a win-win situation because everybody gains and nobody loses. Joint ventures cut through the top heavy expense of finding large numbers of customers from scratch. You don't need to do any market research. You don't need to buy a lot of expensive advertising. You don't need to weed out unqualified clients. Joint ventures drive right to the customer in one swoop. With a joint venture, you make someone else's already captured customers your client's customers. You capitalize instantly on the other's guy's resources, and he's glad to let you do it because he will capitalize on yours.

Joint ventures are a very powerful but underutilized guerrilla marketing strategy. Yet, according to another legendary marketing guru (and mentor to a few of the joint venture business experts in the world today, including myself), Jay Abraham, less than 5% of all business owners use joint ventures properly and most don't know how to use them at all. Joint ventures are successful because of the old business rule that says: "People like to buy from someone they know and trust".

The best and most well-known example of a joint venture is when one company endorses (recommends) someone else's product or services to their customer list with whom they have a relationship and both share the additional profits. This is a win/win arrangement!

For those of you who do not know what a customer list is—it is a list of addresses and/or phone numbers/email addresses that a business owns of all the people who have previously bought from them.

You have probably already been asked your name, address and/or phone number while purchasing something in a store, or your email when surfing the internet. The owners can then communicate with you to try to sell you other things.

Smart business owners regularly send helpful information to their customer lists, thus building a relationship with them. And when they have a good relationship, it's a lot easier to get them to buy more.

The relationship between a business owner and his/her customers is the most valuable asset that a business has, the value of which isn't measured in dollars. However, if you know how to leverage it, it's as good as gold. In fact, when a business is sold, this asset is valued on the balance sheet.

You may not have realized it, but it can cost SIX TIMES AS MUCH to sell to a new buyer than to resell an existing buyer. And, it costs less and less every single time a client buys from the same business again. Eventually, when they buy from the same business enough, all of the money earned is practically pure profit.

On the flip side, using other people's mailing lists allows you to use their assets without paying for them. This way your acquisition cost is ZERO. More of the profit is yours because you don't have to pay for advertising expenses to earn them. This is the true power of Joint Ventures—leveraging other people's resources and assets or even your own for a minimal or sometimes even zero marketing investment upfront.

It is important that you learn about the many benefits of a joint venture as only by knowing them will you realize their worth. As Donald Trump says in his book, The Art of the Deal, *you cannot sell what you do not believe in.*

By learning the several advantages of joint ventures, you will know how important they are for any business. This will empower you with the ability to sell them with efficiency as your words will sound more credible if you actually believe in what you're promoting.

Let's take a look at the benefits of joint ventures:

- Joint ventures will allow you to compensate for your areas of weakness. Your partners will provide the knowledge and the skills that are needed in those areas. For example, you're great with product creation, but you're rather at a loss when it comes to marketing. Your partners in a joint venture will give you the marketing push that you need.

- Joint ventures will allow you to take advantage of the aid of businesses with complementing skills and resources. This exchange of stocks will result in a synergy that can propel all the parties involved to the next level of success.

- Joint ventures can boost your profits very quickly. Two minds are always better than one. What's more if you have three, or five, or even ten working on the same project and wanting to achieve the same 'high level' goals the results will be exceptional.

- Joint ventures are less risky. .This is because the hazards are divided into the number of parties involved, each partner standing to lose only the proportional share of the risks they have undertaken.

- Joint ventures offer great branding potential for FREE. Joining a group of highly respected and established names in your industry will allow your business to acquire some of their luster.

If you have a joint venture with Microsoft for example, you can immediately see how such a JV partnership would do wonders for how people perceive you and your business.

- Joint ventures can build lasting relationships with your partners. Your relationship with them doesn't have to end with the joint venture. You can explore other opportunities with the same people again if things go well the first time around.

These are the points you will need to convey to the partners you are eyeing. Remember, success in the initial stages of doing a joint venture is determined by two things:

1. How well you have established yourself prior to your offer; and
2. How well you present yourself, together with your proposal, for the joint venture.

We will discuss these in full detail in subsequent chapters but for now, suffice it to say that the second factor can only be achieved if you know the exceptional benefits that can be derived from engaging in a joint venture project. This will allow you to present your joint venture proposal in a remarkable way.

Joint Ventures for Solopreneurs

This week I had a conversation with a few coaches and consultants who asked, "Sohail, are joint ventures just for big businesses?" and I replied, "Joint ventures are just what they are called, a venture joining two or more companies with the same goal!"

You see, many solo entrepreneurs work from a home office. Their only connections to the outside world are the internet, e-mail and their telephone. Cold calling, "warm" calling and sending e-mails may seem like the most obvious way to let people know about them and to generate sales but, there's another way that works even better.

An alliance is usually an agreement between two businesses whose services or products complement each other. Each agrees to recommend the other's services to their respective clients and to pay a percentage to the other if the referral results in paying work.

Let's say you're a marketing expert, but you don't do public relations. However, sometimes your clients require public relations as part of their marketing strategy. You meet with several public relations experts who specialize in different fields, but who don't offer your type of marketing services, and you form 3 alliances. A 10% commission is what you agree on for mutual referrals that result in work. Now, both you and your alliance partners are more "full service" providers.

You can offer PR services to your clients and your partners can offer marketing services to theirs through you. In addition, you could add them as "partners" on your website, giving your company the advantage and versatility of an expert team. It's a win–win situation.

A joint venture is formed when you not only have an alliance but you come up with a strategy to find customers together. Suppose you make custom window treatments. You decide to speak to a local fabric shop that specializes in upholstery and window fabric.

If you could be their exclusive referral for customers that need someone to make their fabric into beautiful draperies, and you are willing to pay them a commission for each referral, what happens? They can say they now offer a new value-added service to their customers, which may mean a customer chooses their store above another. You have a steady source of customers. You may even get them to display some of your draperies made with their fabric in your store.

They agree to allow you to advertise in their store, perhaps even offer a workshop, and you'll recommend them exclusively to your clients. You may even advertise together. The possibilities are limitless.

There are numerous ways to put together alliances and joint ventures. Thinking outside the box and being clear about what benefits both parties would receive are essential. As always, getting the agreement in writing is a good idea, as is being sure the person you're dealing with is honorable and reliable.

Try to discover ALL the alliance possibilities that exist for your business. Our custom window treatment business owner above could also contact interior designers, furniture stores, residential real estate agents, home builders, sales offices and even paint stores. So, what are you waiting for? Start today by:

- *Making a list of at least 5 prospective alliance partners.*
- *Making a list of 5 ways the alliance would benefit them and you.*

The Million Dollar Joint Venture Mindset

Having the right JV mindset is the most important element of doing JVs. Without it, you'll find doing JVs frustrating. With it, you'll enjoy the process and the fruits of your labor.

Mindset is very important in this business. If you don't have the mindset of success, then you're destined to fail. Therefore you need to understand the Law of Attraction, and utilize it to enable your mind, body and spirit to work in harmony for attracting and manifesting your desires and goals.

Everyone is capable of success if they put their mind to it, believe in themselves and take action to make it happen—even YOU! The Law of Attraction, when properly utilized, helps enable you with the proper mindset and strategies you require.

Visualization is probably the best means of manifesting something specific using the Law of Attraction. In general, however, you may wish to generate a type of energy around yourself to continually be attracting certain energies that will serve you. For example, using affirmations can be very effective.

If you want to attract the energy of opportunity, then you could use an affirmation such as *"I am the right person, in the right place, at the right time, doing the right things, with the right people!"* This is a great affirmation for manifesting beneficial joint ventures and joint venture partners and is one that I constantly use whenever I speak on stage or at my training programs and retreats.

If you want to attract joint venture opportunities specifically, you could use an affirmation such as *"I am aware of and open to unlimited joint venture opportunities, I am involved in the best 'high-level' joint venture opportunities"*.

When you start doing joint ventures, it is vitally important you start seeing yourself as someone who is on a mission to add value. You want to help others. You know exactly what your partners need. You know exactly what would be of benefit to their clients and you make it happen.

If you want them to feel something, you must feel it first. If you want them to see you as an expert, you must first see yourself as an expert.

CHAPTER 10

HOW TO IDENTIFY POTENTIAL JOINT VENTURE PARTNERS

Coming together is a beginning; keeping together is progress; working together is success

— Henry Ford

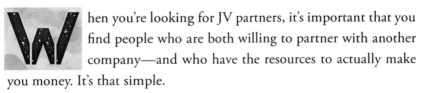 hen you're looking for JV partners, it's important that you find people who are both willing to partner with another company—and who have the resources to actually make you money. It's that simple.

Here's how you identify if you should partner with someone or not:

1. Your potential partner has to be <u>LASER-TARGETED to your audience</u> (your product or your contact base). If this isn't the case, then forget it.
2. Your potential partner MUST <u>have an incredibly active, trusting and money-spending customer base</u> or contact list.
3. Your potential partner <u>MUST be upstanding</u> and have a perfect track-record. Ask for references and "Google" them and their products to check out their reputation online. The odd complaint here and there is to be expected, but if it seems to be a chronic problem, then steer clear.

Tips for finding partners that will guarantee you success from day one:

1. **<u>Go BIG</u>**. Contact the big, wealthy and 'intimidating' companies in your niche first. They are, in most cases, **much more** open to discussing partnerships because they realize that they can easily add to their bottom line by leveraging your product instead of having to research and develop their own.
2. **Look for companies that actually rent their list of qualified buyers or allow targeted third-party offers to their buyers.** In my opinion, this is the best partner as they understand the concept of creative marketing and would be willing to accept joint venture proposals.
3. **Who do you know?** Do you have any industry contacts already (on a 'first-name basis') that you can leverage in your niche? They don't have to be the CEO or MD, or even someone in a 'decision making' role because you can get them to refer you to the key players.

Again, your choice of JV partners for a particular project will ultimately determine the success of it. If you choose highly competent people for your joint venture there is no reason why it would fail.

If the project involves a joint venture for promotional mileage, for example, the partners you should seek are those with sizable mailing lists and an expansive online presence. You simply cannot get a JV partner with a mailing list of 10 subscribers and expect to get any sizeable promotion put together.

Additionally, all of your prospects will want to achieve something grand from the joint venture you're proposing. They simply cannot acquire what they're expecting if you pair them up with people who have less established businesses. This will ruin your efforts and ultimately crumble your credibility as a JV broker as well.

In a nutshell, here are some basic questions you should ask when you choose JV partners for a guerrilla joint venture project:

- Is he/she perfectly qualified for the joint venture you have in mind?
- What can he/she bring to the joint venture that will ensure its success?
- How trustworthy is he/she and how sure can you be that he/she will give his/her full commitment to the success of the project?
- How does he/she compare to the other partners you are considering? Is he/she at the same level of prominence?
- Would your proposed joint venture reap some benefits for the prospects you are considering? Are their businesses compatible with the aspects of the project?
- Are their businesses complementary to each other? Would his/her inclusion be the perfect jigsaw piece to complete the puzzle?

CHAPTER 11

FINDING POTENTIAL JOINT VENTURE PARTNERS

If you want to succeed, you have to forge new paths
— **John D Rockerfeller**

ou will likely have some friends and contacts within your niche. If their target market is similar to yours, then they would be the first people you approach when looking for JV partners.

You will also want to find other business people within your niche or complementary niches wherever similar target markets are found. Contacting and building relationships with these people, even your competitors (which is just one of a wide assortment of marketing tactics used by guerrillas), will be of great benefit to you when you can create some guerrilla joint ventures to involve them in.

Where to Find Potential Joint Venture Partners

Below are the best places to find JV partners:

Existing Mailing or Customer List

This is one of the best places to do deals. Why? Because your customers have already done business with you, they know you, they know your business, and they probably have a **relationship** with you. They will trust you and follow your recommendation if you've built a good relationship with them and you've only sold and endorsed quality products to them.

Newsletter and Publications Directories

Newsletter and Catalog directories are excellent places to find potential partners. Approach these mailing list owners correctly and you will have a very good chance of landing some extremely lucrative deals. Since they send out their publications to their client lists on a regular basis, they often have an excellent relationship with their subscribers.

The Oxbridge Directories of Newsletters and Catalogs is a good place to start as they have plenty of contact lists to choose from at *www.mediafinder.com*. You can either buy it or subscribe to the online service for 3 or 6 months.

You'll find the newsletter or catalog name, if you can advertise in, get them to promote, rent the list, the contact information of the publisher, information about the target audience, size of the mailing list, list rental info, etc.

In the UK the best mailing list directory is from a company called Hilite, run by my good friend Mike Chantry, which has over 25 million names of qualified buyers under management and can be found at *www.hilitedms.co.uk*.

Another directory is the Standard Rates and Data Services (SRDS). The SRDS is a huge list of lists and can be found at *www.srds.com* and will set you back a couple of hundred dollars but it's an invaluable resource for joint ventures.

The UK alternative is called BRAD and is available at *www. bradinsight.co.uk*

The great thing about these books is that the people or businesses who list themselves in these directories do joint ventures regularly— so you probably will not have to educate them on the concept every single time.

How do you JV with a list owner in the SRDS or BRAD? It's simple. If you have a client selling a seminar on how to make more money in 30 days with financial trading, you look up some lists on financial trading (or some other topic similar to the subject of your seminar) and you offer the list owner a commission in return for promoting the seminar to his or her list. That's it. The contact information is there.

Yellow Pages

Most business people listed in the Yellow Pages won't know about this concept, so you should be ready to educate. Nonetheless, it's easy to find complementary businesses for JVs.

Seminars

Seminars have been one of the best places in my experience for finding partners. You can meet and network with a lot of serious and motivated people. The higher the price for the seminar, the more players you will meet. You won't find timewasters at high priced seminars.

Regularly go to seminars in your field and you'll probably be meeting many potential partners, people who have products or big mailing lists. In addition, you get to spend time with them, thus getting to know them and having a better idea whether or not they'd be a good partner.

Search Engines

Go to *www.google.com* and type in the keywords that you are looking for. I will cover this in more detail later.

Discussion Boards

Another great place to find associates is online discussion boards or forums. You can communicate and build relationships with other members, and then propose a deal.

> *www.MillionDollarPartneringClub.com* (the member's forum that I manage)
>
> *www.JVBase.com*
>
> *www.WarriorForum.com/warrior-joint-ventures/*
>
> *http://v3.jvnotifypro.com/community_forums/*

Ezine Directories

Ezine directories are great places to find associates, if you want to JV online. I've listed the best directory below. However, just search 'Ezine Directory' in Google for more resources.

> *www.ezine-dir.com*

Social Network Sites

Firstly *www.LinkedIn.com* is a good social network for business professionals who want to be introduced to and collaborate with other business professionals. Once you create an account, enter keywords related to your target market into the LinkedIn search engine to find potential JV partners.

Two more social networking services that have become extremely popular called *www.Twitter.com* and *www.Facebook.com* have made it easier to connect directly with many of the people with whom you want to do business.

And, depending upon the niche that you are in, you're likely to find tons of social networks that are niche-specific at *www.Ning.com* by using their "Search" feature in the upper right corner of the site.

The mistake most people make when using social networking to find JV partners is that they pitch their JV offer immediately instead of first trying to establish a relationship with their prospective partners.

Social Networking is a pull strategy (meaning you pull people towards you by building relationships) rather than pushing yourself and your message onto people.

Using Google To Find JV Partners

Google is an amazing resource for joint ventures. With a few tricks you can really narrow down your search results and find great opportunities.

Search for keywords related to your niche or complementary niches that share the same target market as you using either *www.google.com* or *www.google.co.uk*. The best partners who'll give you the most marketing leverage will be high traffic website owners, responsive list owners and those who have complementary products and a large customer list.

Authors, experts and famous people can make great JV partners for your product or service.

Here are some Google search tricks for getting better targeted results:

1. Write a list of keywords that most closely match your targeted market.
2. Take each keyword and do the following searches to find suitable JV partners:
   - Search: keyword
   - Search: keyword + news
   - Search: keyword + newsletter
   - Search: keyword + blog
   - Search: keyword + book
   - Search: keyword + ebook
   - Search: keyword + ezine
   - Search: keyword + forum
   - Search: keyword + faq
   - Search: keyword + conference
   - Search keyword + seminar
   - Search: keyword + review

- Search: keyword + resource
- Search: keyword + tips
- Search: keyword +tutorial
- Search: keyword +article

For each list of search results, you'll want to visit the most relevant sites to see if they look like they'd make suitable JV partners.

If they seem suitable for you the next step is to check out their site details at *www.whois.domaintools.com* and find out a bit more about them such as Alexa ranking (which is a website stats tool at *www.alexa. com*), whether they've been blacklisted, how long they've been around, the number of visitors they get, as well as the name and contact details of the owner of the website.

By the time you get through even your first keyword, you should have plenty of potential JV partners to contact. Now place them all on a checklist and rate them as As, Bs and Cs.

As are the most ideal partners with the largest most targeted lists and most targeted high traffic websites. Bs are the second group of potential partners that you'll focus on after the A list. Cs are the ones that are still very important, but with all the contacts you'll have and with the potential money you'll make form the As and Bs, you might want to hire someone later to contact all the C list partners for you.

You'll also want to contact the 'Adwords' text-link advertisers (those listed as "Sponsored Ads" in Google for your keywords), because they're obviously getting traffic and many of them will be experienced marketers because they need to be skilled at optimizing sales conversions in order for PPC advertising to be effective.

Finding JV Partners Using Advanced Google Strategies

This is how you'll be able to find a boatload of additional prospects that you would probably NEVER have found otherwise:

Run a search for your primary keyword(s) in this format:

Inurl:keyword

This will pull up every site that Google indexes with that keyword in its domain name. For example, I just ran a search for the word 'health' as a keyword and my search looked like this:

Inurl:health

The top ten results for that search are VERY different from the top ten listed simply for just the word 'health'

Note: You can also use the format **allinurl:keyphrase** to search for more than one word, such as 'health tips', which would look like this:

Allinurl:health tips

This is very powerful because by searching for domains that use your target keywords, you'll inevitably **find far more potential JV partners** than by simply searching for pages with those keywords in their content.

Once you've established who the main 'go to' sites are that represent your target market, simply go over to Google's advanced search tool which is available at *www.google.com/advanced_search?hl=en*, scroll down to the 'Page Specific Search' box and type in the URL of one of the main 'go to' sites in your niche. Let's pretend that it's 'HealthFreeTips.com'

Google will then display all of the sites that it deems as being 'similar' to that site in terms of content and importance.

CHAPTER 12

APPROACHING AND CONTACTING POTENTIAL JOINT VENTURE PARTNERS

You've got a goal, I've got a goal.
Now all we need is a football team

— **Groucho Marx**

When you take the time to sit down with potential partners and ask them questions, it's amazing to find that they are a lot richer in resources than they think! They may have memberships, under-utilized resources like parking spaces, homes, rooms, equipment that isn't being used, vending machines, inventory that they can't move, products they've started (or books they've written and not published) and never finished, relationships, access, vehicles, boats, aircraft, friends and information that can all be converted into value and therefore into cash by YOU.

Someone else wants what you have! When you talk with partner A and find that he wants what partner B has, you can do a deal. Do a joint venture and sell him partner B's stuff and make a huge profit.

This all sounds great but approaching potential partners is the most intimidating part of doing joint ventures.

The best strategy before contacting potential JV partners is to *build rapport*. This seems obvious, but so many people simply don't bother building relationships.

Here are some ways to build rapport before you contact a potential JV partner:

1. **Help them out with something.** Find something about their business, their website, their ad copy—whatever—that could use a little 'help'. Make sure it's something that you actually have experience with, such as copywriting, etc. Do this without being insulting in any way and you will have just made a new friend. Build on that friendship and keep on helping each other out. When the time comes for you to bring up a proposal, they'll be all ears and 90% of the time, it's going to happen.

2. **Compliments.** Buy their product or get their newsletter or whatever and then send them an insightful comment about what they do. Flatter them, but don't go too 'over the top'. Become a 'regular' contact of theirs and build on that. Then your 'proposals' will simply be an email asking a question and not a structured 'JV proposal' and again 90% of the time, it's going to happen.

3. **Work together.** Invent something to do that would include them somehow. ANYTHING. Think about it for 20 minutes and I guarantee that you'll have some ideas. Set it in motion, make the benefits mutual, do the 'project' and then take it to

the next level. Be creative. The whole key is to understand that in most cases, just like a customer, the relationship needs to be there before they're going to act. You will find some partners that know the JV game well and all they'll want is your proposal, but that's the rare exception.

Contacting Potential JV Partners

Before you actually contact your prospects, you should write a script. Scripts are very, very important. You should write down everything you are going to say to your potential prospects to sell them on the arrangement you have in mind.

This will get your ideas down on paper (or your computer monitor) and you'll be surprised at all the new ideas that you'll add to your script—ideas that may result in success instead of failure.

Below are the best ways to contact JV partners:

Email

Email is practical, easy and cheap. I've had a lot of success using the Internet to send out proposals. Email is a great way to communicate with partners when you are already dealing with them, as opposed to initiating something.

However, business owners usually receive a lot of emails and a lot of them don't bother reading most proposals when they're emailed. That's why you need to think and act outside the box if you want to be really successful and try and pique their interest. Email should never be your only mode of contact and, if used with others, it will be more effective.

FedEx, Recorded Post, etc

This is the BEST way to contact your potential partners. It's a professional approach. It's also rarely used so it will definitely arouse their curiosity.

In other words, your prospects are virtually assured to open your communication, so you have just passed through the first barrier.

One of the best ways for getting past the gatekeeper (personal secretary, etc) is by preparing your joint venture proposal (covered in the next section) and having it delivered by FedEx or courier as opposed to simply using email. Make sure the envelope is addressed to your joint venture prospect by **full name** and mark it **URGENT, Please Hand Deliver.**

Phone

Some people are very good on the phone. If that is true in your case, use it. You can also use the phone to follow up after you send your proposal out. You should also get your partners on the phone after they accept your deal.

However, most people seem to have a knee-jerk reaction when they are cold called and that reaction is not positive. Therefore, always use the phone to follow-up after you have warmed the prospect via email or mail.

If you want to cold call, tell your potential partners in the very beginning that it'll take only a few minutes of their time. The goal of your cold call should be to get an appointment and not try and sell them.

Building a Network of Potential JV Partners

JV deal making entails enjoining people to work on one project and toward some common goals. The key component in such a setup are people, more specifically, the people you know.

You must get to know the people you eventually deal with. Being able to determine what they're good at and where they excel is a skill that a successful JV dealmaker must possess. You will, after all, be the mastermind for the joint venture. You will be introducing people to work together as a team for the fulfilment of the JV deal.

The first step in becoming a good JV dealmaker is building your network. The more people you get to know, the deeper your pool will be when it is time to choose the members of the joint venture you have in mind. Having already made the acquaintance of the people you need beats having to look for people who possess the criteria you require for a certain JV project.

JV dealmakers are also judged by the depth of their network. Prospective partners trust you more if you are able to present them with a sizeable list of people who are potentially up to the task of joining in a joint venture.

It is important to note that every person you meet is a potential joint venture partner!

It doesn't matter if they are a previous customer or client of yours, or a person you have met online, or a member of one of your mailings, or someone you have done business with before -- you must keep their contact details.

Here are some guidelines you might want to follow to help you establish excellent rapport with the would-be members of your potential JV network:

- **Learn how to address people with respect without losing the intimacy of your approach.** People need to feel special. By being polite and treating them with good will, they'll be attracted to your warm personality and therefore your JV project.
- **Try to master the art of remembering names.** People respond more when they are referred to by their name.
- **Always ask for their permission whenever you want to keep their contact details.** A simple "I hope you won't mind my keeping your email address so that I may contact you when I receive some good news" will go a long, long way to making people feel that their presence is valued.
- **Praise their achievements.** People naturally gravitate to individuals who know how to appreciate their efforts. Don't be afraid to give out compliments. Give credit where credit is due.

- **Show some generosity.** You don't have to shower your contacts with expensive gifts. Sometimes, a little greeting out of nowhere will show people that you genuinely care for them. They'll most certainly return your generosity in kind.
- Building and maintaining relationships is the starting point in establishing a network for your JV brokering campaign.
- However, it is not enough to build a list of possible JV partners. In these fast times, there's always that danger that they'll forget about you after some months.
- So, it is important that you remind them of your presence from time to time.

Here are some really effective ways that can help you maintain your prominence in their minds:

- **Send free gifts every now and then.** These may be some products you're offering to your mailing list or a few samples from the latest joint venture deal you're brokering.
- **Inform them of the latest news concerning the industry.** If you read something interesting in a magazine or on a website somewhere, send them the link.
- **Offer to provide reviews or testimonials for their products or services.** Testimonials can help boost their sales. Their prospects will tend to give more credibility to the words of a satisfied party than the sales pitches of the seller. By writing reviews, recommendations, or testimonials for your contacts, they'll feel indebted to you and they will be eager for the next opportunity when they can repay their debt of gratitude.

It would be wise, if not practical, to create a separate mailing list for the members of your network.

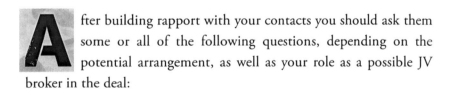

CHAPTER 13

QUESTIONING POTENTIAL JOINT VENTURE PARTNERS

The basic rules of business are the same whatever it might be. The basic requirement is always common sense

— **Sir Charles Clore**

A fter building rapport with your contacts you should ask them some or all of the following questions, depending on the potential arrangement, as well as your role as a possible JV broker in the deal:

1. **Do You Have All The Names and Addresses of Your Customers? Or Do You Have a Mailing List?** If they don't, you'll be limited in the types of joint ventures you can do with them. Unless they have a good product or service you can use

in another JV deal, this prospect probably isn't worth your time or energy.

2. **Is Your Mailing List Composed of Buyers or Visitors/Leads?** Buyers have always been (and always will be) more profitable than leads. Knowing if there are some visitors in that list is VERY important, as they have been known to complain about spam/junk mail, even if they signed up to receive future mailings.

3. **Can You Accept Many More Clients (For Service Type Businesses)?** If so, how many? NOTE: Get a percentage as well as an actual number. The answer to this question will give you an idea of how to structure the deal/mailing. The reason is that it is not to their advantage to have to give a percentage away when they are already booked with customers paying full price.

4. **How Big Is Your Mailing List?** If they don't have enough names, forget it. As a rule of thumb, bigger is better. However, if you are selling a high-ticket product then this is not always the case. I can give you plenty of examples of people who pull in 7 figures per year with mailing lists of less than 2,000 people, all of them being high end buyers. Look for QUALITY here as opposed to QUANTITY, but know what you are working with, too.

5. **How Often Do You Contact Your Mailing List?** Monthly to weekly contact is excellent. Multiple times per day may hinder your chances of reaching the maximum percentage of prospects possible. (Note that for online marketers, it's not unusual to have daily contact, so don't discount a list because contact is frequent. However, more than once per day to once every other day is usually excessive.)

6. **Do They Buy From You Often And, If So, How Often (on Average)?** The more they buy, the better, because they are used to spending money with the owner of the list. Customers that buy often from, or follow the recommendation of, a list

owner are a very good sign because you know that they have a good relationship.

7. **What Is The Percentage of Clients Who Bought More Than Once From You?** Knowing the percentage of repeat buyers is important. It gives you a good idea of the relationship the prospect has with his customers, and tells you whether your potential partner is a savvy marketer that has his best customer's best interest in mind.

8. **When Was The Last Time They Bought Something Similar To What Is Offered In The JV?** The sooner the better but it's better to wait at least 3 weeks after a mailing for a similar product before sending yours out.

9. **How Much Did They Pay Per Product On Average In The Past?** If your product or service is priced along those lines, that's great. If not, you have the choice of lowering your price just for that one deal or dropping the deal altogether.

10. **How Did They Pay?** Try and copy their payment method, if you think it was successful. If you're selling something online, offer both a credit card option and a PayPal option to drastically increase sales.

11. **Do You Have a Money-Back Guarantee? If So, How Long Is It?** If they don't have a money back guarantee, they should. Offering a guarantee is definitely a huge response modifier; in other words, it boosts response. Never partner with anyone who doesn't offer a guarantee. (Note that there is a difference between having a Refund Policy and a Guarantee. Many businesses have a "No Refund" policy, but at the same time, offer a guarantee based on results. This is a creative way of increasing response while at the same time keeping refunds low.)

12. **What is Your Conversion Rate?** The bigger the better. Is it high enough that your efforts will be worthwhile?

13. **Do You Have A Back-End In Place?** If they do, you could try to negotiate a percentage of those sales too. If they refuse, try to get a larger piece of the pie on the front-end.

14. **What Is The Highest-Priced Product That You Have Tried Selling To Your List?** What kind of response did it get?

15. **How Much Does Your Product/Service Retail For? What Is The Mark-Up Or Profit Margin?** If the mark-up is too small, there will be little to split and your income will suffer.

CHAPTER 14

HOW TO AVOID BAD
JOINT VENTURE PARTNERS

*You can't do business with bad people and you can't get hurt with
good people. That's all there is to know*

— **Howard Sheperd**

ot everybody has a good experience with their joint venture
partners, so here are a few pointers to help you avoid bad
potential joint venture partners and joint ventures:

1. **Have your partners sign a Non-Disclosure Agreement (or
    Intellectual Property Rights Agreement)** and have those
    agreements in your possession before telling your partners
    everything. Whether you have them sign something or
    not beforehand depends on the deal and the people you're

working with. If you don't have a non-disclosure agreement, have your lawyer write one for you. Just be sure to explain in-depth what you need it for so he can draft a good one for you. If you can't afford to hire a lawyer, do a search for "free non-disclosure agreements" on Google. Save a few and then simply tweak them to include everything you need.

2. **Have them sign an Agreement (Contract).**

3. **Put in your agreement that you have the right to inspect their shipping records, telephone records, etc** to see if there is a discrepancy between the two. For example, if they got many clients calling to place orders, and they shipped considerably fewer orders, something may be going on.

4. **Never deal with people who seem to be dishonest.** Always listen to your intuition (the little inner-voice or feeling you have) when you're in contact with them. If you have a funny feeling about them, even if it's tiny, forget about it.

5. **Screen your partners beforehand.** If your partner lives in the US, go to www.merlindata.com and if they live in the UK go to www.creditgate.com; this is a service used by private investigators. You can do background checks on all your potential associates before dealing with them. Ask other people in your field if they know them and what they think of them.

6. **Work with people who have good track records,** who are known for their honesty and who have a lot of good testimonials.

7. **If you JV online, there is tracking software available** and other services that will track all the sales and you'll know exactly how many items were sold and what is owed to you.

8. **If you're doing JVs offline and you meet your partner in person,** you can bring a witness with you to the signing of the Agreement.

9. **Offer to pay for everything,** the mailing of the letter and all the other real and provable hard costs, then take those costs out of the gross and divide the rest of the profits.

10. **Go on their website and check for the following things:** see if they include their real names, phone number, mail address, and other contact information. See if they have a privacy policy and a seal from the Better Business Bureau (BBB) or other such quality monitoring programs. Look them up after that to be sure that they really *are* part of that program because some people may just take a seal and put it on their site. Go on www.bbb.org and do a search on their business. If they really are a member of that organization, it's a good sign. Go on Network Solutions at www.networksolutions.com/cgibin/whois/whois and write their domain name in the search box to get their contact info.

11. **If you're the endorser, you may be able to take the orders yourself in order to:** A. Either calculate how many you have received and thus how much is owed to you before sending them (fax or e-mail or whatever ASAP) to the endorser so he can fulfil them or, B. Take the orders, get the money, send the orders ASAP to the endorsee, then pay the endorsee and the broker (if there is one).

12. **If you are the endorser, set the deal up so you can offer a special bonus product/service to every paying customer.** Every time one of them buys something, they have to come see you to get the bonus and that is how you can keep track of the number of sales.

13. **Use a respected third party affiliate tracking service like ClickBank,** or any other service that has a good track record ClickBank will track your sales and then pay you and your affiliates (JV partners) like clockwork.

14. **Do a search on their name with Google.** Doing this may bring up some interesting information and I'm not only talking

about clues about the person's background or work ethics. For example, I just recently researched a marketer I wanted to send a proposal to and you know what? I learned that he only considers JV proposals from people that take the time to call him. If I had contacted him by any other means, I would not have been able to get his attention. Everybody has their rules, and if you don't take the time to find out what they are, chances are you will get it ass-backwards and they won't want to play ball. Do you know what one of my rules is? NEVER call me if we don't know each other; that is NOT the way to approach me.

15. **Only work with warm prospects**. Cold prospects are not only hard to convince to JV with you, they are also riskier partners, as they may not think twice before taking you for a ride. Your main focus should be to build relationships with people, and then make them your offer. It takes longer, but is definitely worth it if you are really afraid of being ripped off. What I said previously about avoiding getting ripped off by list brokers also applies here. If your cold prospect is a friend of one of your contacts, have your contact introduce you directly, or just mention that your friend referred you to your prospect. If the prospect values the relationship they have with your friend, they will be especially careful. In other words, you'll probably be in good hands. If you find someone who has a great reputation, they will probably be a good partner, even if they are a cold prospect. If they make it a point to over deliver, and have been known to bend over backwards to make people happy then, in my opinion, they are almost as good as a warm prospect.

16. **Take things slowly with your partners at first** and drop the deal as soon as you discover that they aren't as trustworthy as you thought.

17. **Talk about getting out before you get in.** Everyone needs to have a clear exit strategy before partnering with others. This won't prevent you from getting ripped off, but it will help in somewhat minimizing the damage. You want to be able to get out with only a few scratches, not after several big hits that could knock you out and ruin you financially.

18. **Don't commit to anything long-term with cold prospects.** Let them know that you are ready to leave the deal *at any time*; you want them to be careful with what they do, and you also want them to understand if you want out. Ideally, if you are dealing with a new partner, avoid JVs that you can't easily get out of—even if you do have an exit strategy.

19. **Set up an escrow account with a bank.** You then instruct the bank to transfer X% of the profits into your special account.

20. **Try to find someone who can recommend a good list broker to you.** Tell them you want to work with someone that they often deal with (and that they have a good relationship with). Then, when you contact the broker, you explain that their good client referred you to them. Remember that they don't know how close you are with their client (your friend) so they'll most likely think twice before ripping you off.

CHAPTER 15

WRITING A MILLION DOLLAR JOINT VENTURE PROPOSAL

It is better to know some of the questions than all of the answers
— James Thurber

In order to participate in joint ventures you need to know how to write killer joint venture proposals. There are 2 ways to write a proposal; you can write a long version or a short one. Which format should you choose?

It depends on the prospect, the method of contact and how busy they are. Many JV proposals are too long. However, if structured properly, your JV proposal will gain you the attention of your prospective JV partner.

In this section, you'll learn a simple formula that you can use to insure that your joint venture proposals get:

1. **Opened**
2. **Read**
3. **Responded To**

As discussed earlier, if you can get your JV proposal into the hands of the right prospective JV partners and it contains the information we outline here, you will dramatically improve your chances of getting your prospects to participate in joint ventures with you which will, in turn, produce great profits for both parties.

Below are the key steps in writing a Million Dollar JV proposal:

1. **Use a captivating headline or opening sentence** that offers your JV partner a great benefit, piques their curiosity and compels them to read your whole letter. If the headline and/or opening sentence is targeted and good enough, they will read the next one, etc. If any part of your offer is not compelling enough, they won't read the rest and you will lose them.

2. **Introduce and present yourself** in such a way as to show them that you are serious, professional and trustworthy.

3. **Make sure you are very clear as to what you want to do.** Specify all the ideas and plans that you have in mind. Being vague will not work in your favor as people are busy.

4. **Make your prospects feel unique and special.**

5. **Make your offer hard to resist.** Remember that you have to sell your joint venture to your potential partner. Write it like a sales letter and **do not** hard-sell them. Pull them into your offer. Incite them to accept your offer.

6. **Explain who you are, how long you have been in business,** what your product or service is like, how many people you have

on your customer list, how responsive they are, your website URL, your conversion rate and any other info that you believe would be of interest to the other party for them to make an educated decision.

7. **Make it look simple.** Keep it organized and logical.

8. **Be sure to make it personal.** This is extremely important. Always use their name. Remember, use your Alexa and Whois online searches and use that information to write your proposal. When you send them an email or a letter with all that hard-to-find information you will probably capture their attention and you will look more professional.

9. **When mailing your proposal, you have to know about the A, B and C piles.** When people receive mail, they always sort it out—they put everything that's personal (or that looks personal) in one pile (the 'A' pile). Then they take what looks more or less important and put it in the 'B' pile to be opened later. The rest (the 'C' pile also known as junk mail) is simply thrown away. So your goal is to be in the 'A' pile—using the FedEx approach as discussed earlier will almost guarantee your proposal gets the right attention.

10. **Be sure to make your JV proposal standout from the rest.** If people are used to splitting profits 50/50 in a joint venture (remember you make your commission on the overall result of the joint venture deal), why not offer more on the first number of sales?

11. **Put the decision makers name in the headline.** The following email subject line has gotten a VERY high response rate for me: "Dear Name, I want to work with you…"

12. **Always offer a guarantee and take away any risk if you can do it.** Try the following in your body copy: *"I want to send you my _____ so you can review it. I am just asking for a few minutes of your time. This is what I mean: spend a few*

moments to skim over my _____ and if it doesn't live up to your expectations, let me know and I will immediately pay you _____ for your efforts".

13. **Put yourself in your prospect's shoes when writing your letter.**

14. **Be sure to write your proposal carefully and to proofread it several times** before firing it off. An excellent way to find mistakes in whatever you write is to read it out loud. Have someone else proofread it also.

15. **If you have any testimonials from other people/businesses that you've joint ventured with, use them.** A strong testimonial that gives figures and results is better. If you can prove that you're honest, hardworking and that you've been very successful in the past it's going to be a big plus.

16. **Be sure to let them know that you are familiar with their business.** If you are subscribed to their e-zine or newsletter, say so. If you've bought from them (which I advise you do to see their buying cycle) and like their product/service, say so but only if you are 100% sincere.

17. **If you partnered with people in their industry, say so.** It gives an instant boost to your credibility. They'll think: "OK, if he/she worked with _____ and _____, he/she must be good or have a viable business proposition. This is called 'Social Proof' and is very powerful.

18. **Give them the impression that they'll get a lot more out of the arrangement than you will.**

19. **Put your proposal in bulleted format and write short paragraphs**—it's easier on the eyes and is more liable to be completely read than a big block of text.

20. **Just like in a well-crafted sales letter, always use your prospect's first name often** and talk to them not at them.

21. **At the end of the letter, tell them what to do and tell them to do it NOW.** If you have deadlines coming up, tell them. If not, they may have a tendency to put it off and you'll lose the deal.

22. **Always use some PSs because they are always read.** Some people read the PSs, first right after the headline. This is your second headline, used to stress the urgency of the situation or the exclusivity.

The Complete Million Dollar JV Proposal Formula

So, to put it all together in a successful formula first of all, compile a list of potential JV partners as discussed earlier.

Then, send them all an initial correspondence piquing their interest. Depending on the niche, your response rate will range from 10% to 50%, give or take, but don't base anything on that. Every niche is different and those figures are simply taken from my experience in the niches that I work with.

Now when someone replies to your initial correspondence, it will be one of two possible responses:

1. **They're Interested.**
2. **They're NOT Interested.**

When this happens (and it will, so get used to it), you can easily 'turn the tables' by asking them two things:

1. *"What would you do if you were me? I'd sincerely appreciate any advice you may be able to offer…"*
2. *"Do you know of anyone else that would be a good fit for this sort of partnership?"*

By doing this, you are going to actually cater to their ego by asking for their expert advice, while at the same time leveraging their rolodex of contacts.

But what you're REALLY after here is their contacts. In most cases, people simply can't resist being 'the teacher' and they'll also feel good about being able to flex their 'influence' by providing you with some of their contacts.

Follow up with the contacts they provide and drop their name when you talk to them. If the contacts they provided had any sort of relationship to the referrer, then you have a very good chance of them wanting to get a proposal from you.

They're Interested

When they respond to your initial correspondence and seem interested, what you're going to do is study not only their response—you're actually going to study HOW they write. Why? Because it's a proven fact that one of the easiest ways to build a rapport with someone is to mimic their mannerisms, expressions and ways of communication—this is widely used in NLP (Neuro Linguistic Programming).

For example if they write in short, 4-word sentences, like:

Thank you for your email/letter
Please call tomorrow sometime.
Tell Linda I'm expecting your call.
—Richard

Then respond in the SAME way...
And if they're classic-style writers then emulate that style also;

Dear Sohail,
Thank you for your email/letter
Yes, we may be interested in forming a mutual partnership.

It would be just as convenient for us if you simply sent your proposal via email.

From there, we can assess the relevance and legitimacy of your offer.

Thank you very much

Regards

Richard Marston

Company Name

Phone Number, Extension

Email

Website

Either way, your goal is to make them feel comfortable with you on a subliminal level. They will see you as an equal and maybe even a potential friend.

So, when they respond with interest, reply to them in a 'mimicking' manner and tell them that you are preparing a detailed proposal specifically for them. This will let them know that you're serious and it's also going to make them anticipate receiving your proposal.

Remember, your prospect will be interested in one of two things— **Money** or **Value**. Their primary interest in a partnership will either be making a lot of money, or adding value for their current customer base. Find out which 'one' they are by taking a look at their previous activities, newsletters and communications with you and gear your proposal towards that 'reason'.

Then end your proposal with a closing paragraph that very briefly sums up the benefits for them as well as the 'next step' for them to take. Just like a well-crafted sales letter, you need to have a 'call to action'—which in this case is going to be making a decision and getting back to you.

Just like your JV proposal, the negotiations process and the structuring of the final deal has to be as simple and clearly laid out as possible. Your goal should be to get the best win/win arrangement possible. Before you enter into negotiations, always remember that everything is negotiable and just follow the tips below:

1. **Understand your potential JV partner and what they really want.** Once you know this, then you know which 'buttons' to press. Listen very closely to how they react to certain things you say. This will show you what to stress and what to leave alone.

2. **Don't be a push-over.** Especially when you're dealing with larger companies you'll find that they've been conditioned to dealing with desperate and 'small-minded' businesspeople.

3. **Know exactly how much you can offer them BEFORE you begin negotiations.** When dealing with bigger companies it's common practice to offer less upfront than you're actually willing to part with. Your potential JV partner will usually counter that initial proposal with a request for more and then you'll meet in the middle and everyone's happy.

4. **Have a specific ACTION PLAN.** Nobody cares about theories, ideas or the word 'potential'. They want to see real numbers and proven strategies and they want to know EXACTLY how this can be 'actionable' should a partnership occur.

5. **Set a Date.** Make it clear that you mean serious business and don't let them 'put it off'. As much as possible, try to arrange a solid, concrete start date for the JV. Communicate regularly about it and act as if they're going to move ahead with it as well, but without being pushy. Be sensible, but understand that your confidence in this area can literally almost 'strong arm' a fence-sitting prospect into an action-taking JV partner.

CHAPTER 16

CLOSING THE
JOINT VENTURE DEAL

In business, you don't get what you deserve, you get what you negotiate

— **Chester L. Karrass**

ome people would not participate in a joint venture unless they had a contract while others fiercely refuse to use them, preferring instead to rely on a handshake. The choice really is yours to make.

This section has been provided for those of you who have the need for JV contracts and other related agreements.

<u>PLEASE NOTE</u>: Any and ALL material provided to you is supplied as an example *ONLY* and does **NOT** constitute legal advice. You should consult your own attorney to create any legal document you use in your business, including any legal documents you use in joint ventures.

Below are some tips on setting up the actual JV and agreement:

1. **Make it Irresistible.** This means that you will, in many cases, need to be very generous with the upfront profits of the deal. Keep in mind that JV's produce money, customers and **lifelong** profits for ZERO RISK. Besides, the real profits are always on the 'backend'.

2. **Go for the long-term profits.** Instead of solely going after the 'one off' type of deals, develop a long-term strategy that will make both you and your JV partner more money for years to come. We will discuss types of joint ventures in a following section.

3. **Non-Disclosure Agreements.** Before you start negotiating and sharing information with your prospect about your business, you may want to have them sign an 'NDA'. This protects you legally in case they decide to rip off your trade secrets, strategies, sales processes, IP (intellectual properties) or even your product. This is not always required but it is certainly recommended— especially if you are working with a totally new JV partner that you have no pre-existing relationship with.

4. **Use a Specific JV Agreement.** Only start drafting the agreement once the deal has been solidified with a 'handshake' of some kind, whether physical, figurative or virtual. It's a good idea to send an email summarizing the agreement in principle between you while you are working on formalizing the written contract.

Making the Joint Venture Deal Successful

The longer your JV partners take between accepting the deal and actually carrying it out, the more time they have to doubt and question and come up with objections, and the more chances you have of your JV deal not being successful.

To increase the chances of getting your JV contract signed apply the tips below:

1. **Spend time communicating with them.** Build a relationship with them, or if you already know them well, spend some time and effort deepening that relationship.

2. **In writing, clearly outline the expectations of your JV partner as well as your own expectations.** Other people's expectations of who we are play a major role in the actions we undertake. For example, if you let them know that you see them as the kind of person that follows through, who is action-orientated, it will definitely affect the way they act around you—as well as how they handle the JV deal.

3. **Get them to commit to a specific time-frame and come up with a deadline.** You also want to know how much time it will take them to carry everything out.

4. **Keep them posted at all times and track EVERYTHING.**

Carrying Out Due Diligence

As a JV dealmaker, you're also responsible for the convenience of the JV partners you have managed to invite into the joint venture. Hence, you have to do everything in your power to make sure that things run smoothly for them.

This includes helping them conduct their due diligence.

Due diligence is a careful scrutiny of the proposal to appraise the risks involved and to determine the feasibility and profitability of the proposal. It is also a way to measure the depth of the implications of the business decisions that will eventually be made throughout the course of the undertaking.

This will require some information.

As the middleman you will be asked to provide information to the members of the joint venture. Such information may be in the form of:

- Personal details and background of the other partners, as well as their businesses.
- Qualifications of the other partners, as well as their businesses.
- The most appropriate business structure for the joint venture and a commitment to respect it once it is established.
- The terms and conditions that should be followed throughout the duration of the joint venture.
- The designation of tasks between the JV partners and phase timetables.
- A profit-sharing scheme for the participants. Make sure that your share is represented as discussed in an earlier section.
- An exit strategy for the partners, in the event that the joint venture eventually proves detrimental to their interests. Exit clauses should be handled with care and should be based only on legitimate and justifiable grounds.
- A system for sharing risks and expenditures, like ways on how to deal with losses, how to compensate people who render services, and how to pay for supplies necessary for the joint venture.

Maximizing the Joint Venture

Maximizing profit in any JV deal comes down to establishing and optimizing a system of selling. Here are two ways to easily maximize a typical joint venture so that you and your JV partners will earn as much money as possible:

1. **Think Long Term.** Too many JVs are simply a one-time deal where a company recommends a related product to its list of customers in exchange for a cut of any sales generated. While

this is a great way to kick off a partnership and make some instant sales, you should go much further and turn it into a 'lifetime' of profits rather than a one-time deal.

2. **Pre-Test Your JV campaign.** By using proven promotional copy your sales could increase by literally ten times or more. Split test headlines and offers on a smaller scale first before you decide to roll out your joint venture.

The Key Elements of a Successful Joint Venture

Before any joint venture can be successful many elements must be perfect. But the key elements originally taught to me by one of my millionaire mentors are those called the "golden keys", which include having:

1. **A great product or service.**
2. **An even better Unique Selling Proposition (USP).**
3. **A package to tie 1 and 2 together (this is your marketing plan, promotional materials or your website).**
4. **Joint Venture Partners.**

If the first 3 elements exist, the last component (Joint Venture Partners) is the easy part of the equation. When organizing any joint venture, more than 90% of the effort must be spent getting the first three components ready.

First, take a look at your product or service. Is it good? Does your product or service solve a burning issue for the purchaser or does the purchaser have a burning desire for your product or service? Is the product or service truly needed or desperately wanted? Is there a market for your product? Where?

All products and services can benefit from joint venture deals. Whether the deal serves to make a product or service better, to create add-on products or services, or to improve sales of a product or service, there is some type of benefit to be realized for the product or service from a joint venture deal.

As a JV dealmaker, you will often see the profit potential where your clients don't. You can help them find and create a USP for their product or service.

Depending on your particular product or service, there may be other key elements that are vital to the success of a joint venture deal but, without a good product or service, a good USP, a tremendous marketing plan and promotional materials, the other elements simply won't work.

Closing the Deal

I could write a whole book on the *'Art of Negotiating and Closing Deals'* but I'm going to cover just enough for you to get started. One of the richest men in America, *J Paul Getty,* said it best when he quoted, *'My father said: "You must never try to make all the money that's in a deal. Let the other fellow make some money too, because if you have a reputation for always making all the money, you won't have many deals."'* So, tip number one—don't be GREEDY!

There are 4 main phases of negotiating:

1. **Planning**
2. **Debating**
3. **Proposing**
4. **Bargaining**

The Planning Phase

This is where you identify your supporting arguments that justify your objectives and the arguments that the other party may use against them. Ask yourself how you will counter their arguments? What strengths and weaknesses do you take to the negotiating table? How can you maximise your strengths and minimise your weaknesses? What are the strengths/ weaknesses of other party? What will be your opening gambit and how will you present it? Also, with regard to timescales—how much time is there to negotiate and how imperative are deadlines?

The Debating Phase

Here you need a positive powerful opening—confident body language and tone to break the ice and discuss neutral topics for building rapport quickly. You also need to cover: Why we are here? What we are going to do and how long will it take? Emphasise the need for agreement at the outset and listen to what the other party says and how they say it. Observe non-verbal signals and sit where you can see everyone. If you are with one other person, sit apart so you are 2 voices and exchange information through statements.

The Proposing Phase

Here you need to decide whether you will speak your proposal first or respond to the proposal from the other party. Put forward your proposal with as little emotion as possible and make sure you leave room for manoeuvre. Avoid—'wish', 'hope', 'would like'—this is not assertive language. When you make and consider proposals it means you are moving towards a jointly agreed solution. Proposals consist of 2 elements: the condition plus the offer. Both the condition and the offer can be couched vaguely but it is better to state your condition first. *For Example: 'If you change your terms of business, then I could consider some amendments to our payment schedule.'*

The Bargaining Phase

At this final stage you need to be prepared to make concessions, offer the smallest concessions first—you may not need to go any further. Compromise without losing face, if you have had to backtrack on a point you had as your final position you could say *'Since you have changed your position on... I may be able to change mine on...'* Make eye contact to emphasise that each concession is a serious loss for you. Do not ignore issues in order to speed up negotiations and record fully all agreements finalized at the close of negotiations.

When it comes to closing there are only 3 closes you should use:

1. **Summary Close**
2. **Adjournment Close**
3. **Final, Final Offer Close**

The Summary Close
This basically summarizes the details of the conditions and the offer, and then just asks for the agreement.

The Adjournment Close
Useful where there remains some small differences. It gives both parties time away to consider the final agreement.

The Final, Final Offer Close
Make it clear that this is your final, final offer by choosing the right words, tone and body language. Create an atmosphere of decisiveness by gathering your papers together as though getting ready to leave.

Dealing With Difficult Negotiators
Do not let their behaviour affect the outcome—that is what they want. They know if they behave in this way they will get what they want because the other party will back down. Do not react to their behaviour—that is what they want. Stay focused on the benefits and outcome. You need to ignore their behaviour, this is what they choose—not you. Concentrate on the outcome and do not let their behaviour influence you away from this.

PART FOUR

JOINT VENTURES
AT WORK

CHAPTER 17

TYPES OF
JOINT VENTURES

*Knowing is not enough, we must apply. Willing is not enough,
we must do*

— Johann von Goethe

Yellow Pages

ook in the Yellow Pages and find several businesses that sell quality products that have a high mark-up. Send them a personal letter by FedEx or Courier and explain that you want to share with them an idea that you believe will make them a tidy profit. They have no risk whatsoever and no initial investment.

Tell them to contact you as soon as possible.

The day after or so, follow up with all of those who haven't contacted you and ask them if they have received and read your letter.

Propose to meet them and be sure to say that it will take just a few minutes of their time.

Ask beforehand if they have a customer list. If they don't, you can still JV with them by having them offer their product to another JV partner's list.

Once you meet ask them the usual questions:

- How many names do they have on their customer list?
- How often do they buy?
- Do they contact their customers regularly?
- How much are they used to paying?
- What is their product or services profit margin?
- Are their products or services selling well?
- Which ones are selling best? Etc.

If you are satisfied with the prospect and the arrangement looks like it has the potential to be profitable, do the deal. You have 2 options: either you sell their stuff to someone else's mailing list or you can sell their stuff to their own customers using proven promotional copy in discount coupons and offers.

Online

You find someone that has a great product. The person has a lot of raving testimonials on their website. Copy their website URL and go to *www. alexa.com/siteinfo/XXX* (replace the XXX with their URL). You'll find some interesting statistics on their website and business.

Another website you should go to get information on your prospect's business such as the decision makers contact details and their competitors, etc, is: www.whois.ws and also *www.compete.com*.

If you have any doubt as to whether a JV prospect serves the right audience, visit *www.Quantcast.com/XXX* (again, replace the XXX with your prospect's URL). You'll find interesting information about the demographics of their visitors, the other sites their visitors are frequenting, the keywords their visitors are searching for, etc.

As the dealmaker, ask the JV partner to give you an affiliate code to track the orders. If they don't have an affiliate program get them to sign up (or maybe arrange to do it yourself) to the following online program to track sales: *www.1shoppingcart.com*

I was approached by a lesser known marketer to connect him with a very well-known marketer to broker an online joint venture which ultimately ended doing just under $4 Million in sales.

Licensing

Licensing is my favorite because you can be making money almost immediately after you buy or own the rights to those things that have been tested and proven.

And what's great about the fact that it's already been tested is that you don't need to spend all that time, money and energy to test the things. It's already been done for you so you're leveraging all that time and energy.

This is an easy and low risk way to make lots of money when you choose your product to license well, especially with JVs.

You should find a product (also look overseas) that is of great quality, sells for a lot, has been proven, has a very high demand, still has a life, is targeted towards a market that is huge, that has money to buy it and that are easy to reach.

You charge people a fee for the rights to your product and you make money from the royalties hands-free. You can either charge for the exclusive or non-exclusive rights to your product/s.

A few years ago I had the pleasure of meeting a licensing legend at his $25 million waterfront mansion in Jupiter, Florida while I was in the US. That person's name was John Osher—creator of the 'Spin Pop' and 'Spin Brush' which he licensed and sold to Proctor and Gamble for $475 Million!

The introduction was through a fellow joint venture broker and friend of mine, Ronak Ganatra (a great joint venture broker—seek him out!). As we pulled up at a private country club estate the security guard opened the enormous gates and we drove up the never-ending driveway. Having arrived at a truly magnificent mansion overlooking the waterfront, we walked up to the front door and rang the bell.

Now most of you who know my story of making millions just using joint ventures and then losing millions before eventually working my way back from just one 7-figure licensing JV deal might guess that I was very excited to be meeting someone who did a 9-figure licensing deal!

John invited us into his beautiful home and to his private office (which looked like a command centre at NASA). The first question John asked was, "What deal do you have for me to look at?" If only I did have a deal ready to show! After having a great conversation and picking his brains, I promised John that if I came across the 'BIG' one again, I would reserve it just for him!

So how did he do it?

I want to first make clear that John's story is FAR from the typical entrepreneur's experience. However, it's relevant nonetheless because many of the skills he used to bring his product to market, despite having sophisticated design teams, established contacts, and sufficient funds, are the same ones you must master.

John knew the potential market for such a product was enormous— every sex, race, religion, creed brushed their teeth, right? But because the retail price of electric toothbrushes was between seventy and eighty dollars, the product simply wasn't affordable.

But John had the technology to create a new electric toothbrush— he would apply the same technique utilized by the inexpensive toy candy twirler to a toothbrush.

It's a good thing he didn't give up. John has enjoyed the type of lucrative success most people can't even comprehend and most of it is due to his persistence in demonstrating that the Spin Brush was a desirable product.

John performed market tests in Meyers stores in Michigan and Ohio—the Spin Brush sold about seven per day. The leading electrical toothbrush at the time sold two a week. He also ran tests with consumers directly. The brush received the highest customer satisfaction and support, ever. It was this specific type of evidence that eventually led John to sign with Proctor and Gamble.

Below are some lessons I learnt from John Osher:

- *Must set price right.*
- *Spent 6 years after undergrad as a carpenter to gain skills.*
- *Invented the Baby Gym and eventually sold it to Gerber.*
- *Left Gerber to start a toy company.*

At one point he got stuck with too much inventory and investors wanted out. He went through hell and ended up getting a divorce. After 6 months of being on his knees, things turned around. The company wasn't a huge success, but he wouldn't say it was a failure either.

With most of his companies, he had critical times that required hard decisions. He created interactive candy and eventually sold the toy company to Hasbro and became VP of Nothing. He left Hasbro and retired for a year.

Got together and formed a joint venture with a bunch of inventor friends and thought up things that people use every day. They came up with a list of 100 things.

As an entrepreneur, you have to keep things simple. What is your breakeven? How much do you have to sell to make a 15% profit? ALL entrepreneurs should know the basic financials inside out. He has several more ideas in the pot and a few consumer products coming out soon (disposable electric razor?)

One Final Note—some people have asked whether or not to disclose the partnership to the client. Sometimes it's obvious that you are referring a client to your alliance partner, as in the case of the drapery maker and the fabric store. If it's not so apparent, you may want to simply inform your client that you will be working with your alliance partner who is an expert in their field.

I just recently completed another 6 figure deal to license my joint venture training material to an organization that runs networking groups for their small business members.

Reactivating Inactive Buyers

Customer attrition is the amount of customers that businesses lose every year, usually around 20%. Businesses are so busy looking for new customers that they lose existing customers and don't even know it.

It costs 5 times as much to get a new customer as it does to resell an existing customer, so you can make easy money from reactivating lost customers.

You can show business owners how to reactivate dormant customers, for a percentage of the profits. Many offline business owners have customer lists. However, they often don't know how to market to it. Show them they can profit from it and take a percentage of the profits.

Unconverted Leads

Company A gets 5,000 call-in leads a month. They convert 15% of them. What should they do with the other 4,250 leads? It cost them a lot of money to generate those leads!

You take the unconverted leads that Company A doesn't sell and sell them to Company B and get paid a percentage on sales made and split the income with Company A.

This is very simple, EVERY salesperson has unconverted leads. They get paid a lot to get them but for some reason they didn't buy. Now you can turn those leads into ready cash.

A great example of how we did this in one of my previous companies was to basically take unconverted leads from companies who were selling instructor-led computer training courses and sell them our online computer training courses instead. We also gave them our unconverted leads for people who weren't interested in online computer training courses but wanted instructor-led computer training courses.

Distribution

You find a distributor that has an existing sales channel and then find a good quality targeted product. You take a cut on every sale made on both sides. Simple deal.

Another thing you can do is negotiate exclusivity if the product owner does not have some kind of affiliate program in place. *Control the distribution and you control the money!*

Product Creation

You can approach people with great products that aren't electronic and offer to transcribe or re-purpose their product for them (like my $1.5M deal).

That way they can also sell it as an electronic product to JV partners you find. Ask for a percentage of sales on that. *You can create 6 and 7 figures with this strategy.*

Upselling

Show other companies how they can upsell other products or services to increase the average unit of purchase.

You go out and find the other products for a cut. *Every company needs an upsell strategy!*

CHAPTER 18

OFFLINE JOINT VENTURES

Talent is what you possess; genius is what possesses you
— **Malcolm Cowley**

elow are some good examples of offline joint ventures:

Offline Joint Venture Example 1

Sarah sells Avon and her friend Amy owns a health spa for women. Their two products are both geared towards women, or more specifically, the beauty of women. Amy and Sarah see a way to help each other out in their businesses. First Sarah leaves a number of monthly catalogues for her Avon business at Amy's spa.

She also provides Amy with samples of products that women who visit a health spa would be interested in. Amy supplies Sarah with discount cards and Sarah gives each of her customers one of these discount cards which entitles them to a free visit and a discount off their first year of membership.

Both women find that business has vastly increased and both are happy with the arrangement. *As a Deal Maker, can you find two complementary businesses like this and set it all up? If so, then you could take a percentage of the sales that Sarah makes of her Avon products through Amy's spa, and you can also make a percentage of the sales that Amy makes from selling spa services to Sarah's Avon customers.*

Offline Joint Venture Example 2

Robert is a joint venture broker and approaches 25 different businesses to get each one to offer him a sample or taste of their business to give away. For example, Business 1 is an accountant who gives Robert a coupon for a free consultation worth $200. Business 2 offers samples of its products worth $50 and Business 3 offers a free single room carpet cleaning coupon. These valuable coupons and samples come with the understanding that, if the sample of free consultation or service results in business, Robert gets paid an on-going commission on ALL resulting business for a certain period of time. Robert is now armed with hundreds and even thousands of pounds worth of coupons, gift certificates and samples that didn't cost him anything.

Robert now approaches different businesses and tells them that if they gave him a list of inactive customers and he had a proven way to ethically bribe them and entice them back to reactivate these customers with his "Welcome Home" package worth hundreds of pounds along with a proven scripted marketing approach, would the businesses be prepared to pay him a percentage of the on-going business, which they wouldn't have had, over the last one or two years? *Not only does Robert get a percentage of the reactivated customers but also a percentage of the sales from ALL the businesses providing the coupons!*

Offline Joint Venture Example 3

Carol owns a flower shop, but her customers often ask for specialty gift baskets. She doesn't personally know anyone who does gift baskets and decides that this is not something she wants to take on herself. She needs someone who can do beautiful specialty gift baskets. She does know someone who has done joint venture deals in the past, so she contacts them and gets the name of their joint venture broker. Carol contacts the broker and tells the broker what she needs—to be able to supply her customers with gift baskets when they request them. She expects, of course, to keep some of the proceeds from the sale of the gift basket herself. The broker contacts gift basket makers in Carol's area and finds one that agrees to work with Carol.

Now, when one of Carol's customers asks if they do gift baskets she can tell them yes. She takes the order, contacts the gift basket maker, has her delivery person pick the basket up and then has it delivered to the recipient. The gift basket maker is then paid monthly for all gift baskets that have been done for Carol's customers and Carol makes a profit as well. *The joint venture broker gets paid their agreed percentage of the sales as well—everyone is happy.*

CHAPTER 19

ONLINE JOINT VENTURES

In the online world, it's not what you've got, it's when you've got it
— **Jonathan Waldern**

Below are some good examples of online joint ventures:

Online Joint Venture Example 1

Albert has an e-book about arthritis and how it affects an afflicted person's daily life. Steve, who sells an herbal remedy for arthritis, is found and contacted by Albert for a review of the e-book and a testimonial. Steve reads the book and sees that his product ties in nicely with the content of the book. He talks with Albert about a joint venture deal. Albert agrees to promote Steve's herbal remedy within the e-book in exchange for a commission on the sale of the remedy. Neither of them has any good marketing skills but Steve finds a joint venture broker who has excellent online marketing skills.

The joint venture broker agrees to help make the joint venture deal a success by marketing the e-book for a percentage of the sales. *All three of these people work together to make sure that the JV deal is marketed in the best possible way.* <u>The joint venture broker takes a percentage from the sales of the e-book AND a percentage of the sales of the herbal remedy</u>. Talk about a win-win-win relationship!

Online Joint Venture Example 2

John wants to build a membership website to help people learn how to use their computers and the internet better. Unfortunately, he doesn't have the programming skills that will be necessary to make the site do what he wants it to do. He talks to a friend who recommends another person, a programmer named Heather. Heather has the skills to make John's website do whatever he wants it to do, but her rates are high and John doesn't have that kind of money to spare.

John's plan is to sell various affiliate products from the website. In his quest for those affiliate-related products and services, he meets Jake. Jake has created an online course for people who need instruction on how to use the Internet effectively. Some may see Jake as John's competitor, but John doesn't see it that way; he may not have the programming skills but he has marketing skills that are out of this world and John doesn't.

John approaches Jake, making the initial contact through email. He tells Jake about his vision for his site and how he thinks they can help each other out. They work out an arrangement. John will include Jake's course at a discounted rate to his website subscribers and give Jonathan a percentage of the membership fees to make up the difference in price for Jonathan's product. The two of them approach Heather. They work out an arrangement with her as well, offering her a percentage of membership fees for a specified period of time after the launch of the site.

They all sign formal agreements that lay out what each is responsible for and how each member of the joint venture will be compensated.

Heather builds the site and it is remarkable. The three of them go over Jonathan's course and find additional related affiliate products to include in the course. John starts promoting the site and everyone is very happy with the results. *As a deal maker, can you find three complementary businesses like these and set it all up?*

Online Joint Venture Example 3

Tariq is a consultant for start-up online businesses. He helps those who want to start their own online business through the entire start-up process, holding their hand all along the way. In fact, he gets them through the entire first year, for a very large fee. He is good at what he does and he is worth every penny, but getting clients isn't easy. He knows if he can partner with other people he would get more business.

He contacts a joint venture broker and tells him what he wants to accomplish. This particular joint venture broker knows people who have huge mailing lists of people who want to start their own businesses. He matches Tariq with these list owners and starts setting up teleseminars for the list owners. Tariq will be on each of these calls.

The list owners start sending out pre-sell letters to their lists and people start registering for the calls. The pre-sells are all huge successes and the call spots are all filled. Tariq goes on the calls with each individual list owner and starts discussing how to go about starting up an online business. He also explains what his consultation services can do to help people just starting out. The calls are very successful and all of his consultation spots are quickly filled and there is now a waiting list.

The list owners are all given a percentage of his fees and the broker gets a percentage as well. The entire joint venture deal was so successful that the joint venture broker contacts Tariq again and suggests that he do another joint venture deal with the same list owners to do a paid series of calls with the list subscribers. Again, everyone enjoys success with each member of the joint venture making a percentage of the call profits. *The joint venture broker was very successful in finding the appropriate list owners to meet Tariq's goals, and of course Tariq, the list owners, the subscribers, that participated in the calls and the JV broker all benefited.*

PART FIVE

YOUR MILLION DOLLAR JOINT VENTURE PLAN

CHAPTER 20

39 QUICK START
JOINT VENTURE IDEAS

Do or do not, There is no try

— Yoda

Examples of Joint Venture Partnerships To Get You Started

Please find below 39 Quick Start Joint Venture Ideas to get you started:

- Beautician / Tanning Studio / Hairdresser / Fashion Boutique
- Bookstore / College
- Bridal Ware Store / Photographer / Printer / Limousine Service / Florist
- Business Success Book Seller / Business Consultant / Accountant
- Camera Store / Travel Agent / Computer Store
- Car Accessories / Car Dealership / Insurance Broker
- Car Detailer / Car Dealer / Car Body Shop / Car Wash

- Chemist / Complementary Medicine Practitioners
- Chiropractor / Health Supplement Vendor
- Computer Dealers / IT Support Companies
- Construction Company / Architect / Interior Designer / Landscapers
- Children's Clothing Store / Photographer / Toy Shop
- Decorator / Carpenter / Builder / Plumber
- Dry Cleaner / Fashion Boutique / Men's Outfitters
- Estate Agent / Security and Alarm Company
- Farm Equipment / Fertilizer Company
- Fashion Store / Jeweler
- Film Developer / Camera Store / Travel Agency
- Florist / Funeral Director
- Graphic Designer / Printer Graphic Design / Ad Agency
- Gym / Bicycle Store / Martial Arts Instructor
- Insurance Broker / Accountant
- Italian Restaurant / Italy Travel Packages
- Jeweler / Hotel / Hairdresser / Posh Restaurant
- Landscaper / Garden Centre
- Newsletter / Information or Book Products
- Newsletter / Investment Service
- Office Equipment / Office Supplies
- Pet Boarding / Pet Groomer / Pet Products / Vet
- Photographer / Bridal Ware Store
- Plumber / Builder / Electrician
- Printer / Graphic Designer
- Publishing Business / Software Business
- Removals Company / Storage Facility / Relocation Adviser
- Restaurant / Radio Station / Wine Retailer
- Software Business / Catalog Company
- Solicitor / Financial Adviser / Accountant / Management Consultant

- Toy Shop / Entertainers / Clowns
- Tree Surgeon / Firewood Vendor / Landscaper

CHAPTER 21

YOUR JOINT VENTURE CHECKLIST

Who does chance favour? The prepared mind

— **Louis Pasteur**

1. **Establish Your Desired Outcome and Write It Down**
   What do you want to specifically get out of the joint venture?
   Make sure to have specific and action-orientated goals for your
   joint venture including a realistic time frame for execution.

2. **Define The Target Market**
   Look at your own clients and then choose the clients you want
   to attract by analysing your target market for buying habits and
   trends. Think about what other products or services they also
   buy apart from the ones you sell.

3. **Identify Potential Joint Venture Partners**

   Look at potential joint venture partners who also serve your target market and offer complementary products or services.

4. **Determine The Type of Joint Venture and Share**

   Do you want to do a standard profit share, reciprocal, or both? Would the joint venture be online or offline?

5. **Create Your Action Plan**

   Now you have your potential joint venture partners and joint venture you need to create your action plan. Lucky for you there is already a 7-day action plan you can follow in the next chapter.

6. **Contact Potential Joint Venture Partners**

   Use the strategies and tactics in this book to contact your potential joint venture partners and secure a meeting to emphasize your joint venture proposal and why they should partner with you.

7. **Close the Deal**

   Decide whether you want to close the deal on a hand-shake or contract (I prefer contracts) and make sure that each party knows their roles and responsibilities.

8. **Implement and Manage the Joint Venture**

   Put the necessary foundations and tracking in place to make sure the joint venture is successful and manage the joint venture partner/s to make sure roles and responsibilities are being carried out according to your joint venture agreement.

CHAPTER 22

YOUR 7 DAY
JOINT VENTURE
ACTION PLAN

The only thing that really matters is taking action, If you can do that, the rest comes very easily

— Sohail Khan

Your Quick Fire Joint Venture Proposal Template

lease find below a Quick Fire Joint Venture Proposal Letter template that you can use to secure your first joint venture partner within 7 days:

Dear {Prospect},

I was recommended to contact you as someone who is open to new partnership opportunities. I am currently promoting {Product Or Service} and I would like to propose a partnership that will make us both a steady stream of income. {Product or Service} has a great reputation in the marketplace and with the excellent (Commission % 55%-75% Recommended) commission I am prepared to offer you there is a lot of potential for the both of us.

I have sales materials, etc, ready for you as well as links to track your commissions.

If you are interested, please e-mail me back and I will send you a free (Copy Or Trial) of (Product Or Service) so you can examine the quality for yourself along with some testimonials of some of our current satisfied clients.

I look forward to hearing from you soon and please take a minute to review the sales letter to familiarize yourself with (Product Or Service).

(URL To Product Or Service)

To Your Success,

(Your Name)

(Your email Address)

(URL To Product)

Your 7 Day Joint Venture Action Plan

Day 1

Open a blank text document and go to your favourite search engine and type in keywords relating to the product or service you are promoting. Quickly visit sites that relate to your product or service and take down names and e-mail addresses of sites that look like profitable JV partners until you have 15. That's it for today!

Day 2

Open your document and do the same thing today as yesterday except use a different search engine and different keywords to find 15 more potential JV partners. That's it for today!

Day 3

Write up an excellent joint venture proposal to send out by e-mail. Use the quick fire template above that is very effective. Just add in the parts that ask for your information and you're set! Get your JV proposal edited with all of your information and save it into a text document. That's it for today!

Day 4

Today is pretty easy. Analyze your costs and offer the highest percentage you can to your potential JV prospects. I recommend 55%-70%, which sounds like a lot but these JV partners will be doing all the work so this is money you never would have seen and with no additional work for you.

Also offer a free copy of your product upon request. Don't send it out with the initial proposal, make them raise their hand and say "Yes! I'm Interested!" Take the next few minutes to go over your letter and make it as appealing as possible to the potential JV partner. That's it for today!

Day 5

Open your e-mail program and paste the JV proposal you have now perfected into the body. Insert a headline such as, "Paul—A Joint Venture Opportunity For Your Consideration" into the subject line. Always personalize the subject line and opening line such as "Dear Paul".

This shows you didn't just load everyone into a mass mailer and blast an ad out. Now open your Joint Venture prospect database and plug in the name and e-mail address of your fist prospect into the e-mail. Repeat the above procedure until you've sent to your database of 30 prospects. That's it for today!

Day 6

Today you should start receiving requests for the free copy of the product you offered in your initial proposal. Send it to your prospect right away and thank them for their consideration of your offer. You may also get requests for links to promote your product today depending on the eagerness of your prospects to get started.

Day 7

Today just keep sending the product and affiliate links out as requested and you'll have yourself a powerful sales-force promoting your product while you sit back and watch the orders come in!

FREE JOINT VENTURE VIDEO TRAINING

(Worth $397)

Get access to the Million Dollar Partnering Club

➡ **Get FREE video training from Sohail** featuring LIVE seminar recordings, joint venture and business growth training online, updated regularly.

➡ **Attend LIVE training webinars,** hot seats and mentoring from Sohail and his team of certified Joint Venture Brokers in our monthly member's only network.

➡ **Post questions on the MDPC Forum Boards**, get detailed answers to all your joint venture and business growth questions instantly.

➡ **Get insider tips**, joint venture opportunities and VIP events in our monthly member's only network where you also get direct access to other potential joint venture partners.

➡ **Get access to beginner and advanced training on Joint Ventures**—a comprehensive set of interactive training modules and resources online.

➡ **Get access to joint venture agreement examples**, templates and resources in our member's area that you can use to create your own Million Dollar Partnering success stories.

➡ **Chat LIVE and interact** with other members using our unique online training platform.

REGISTER FOR YOUR FREE BONUS TRAINING AT:
MillionDollarPartneringClub.com

Also check out the Guerrilla Marketing and Joint Ventures official web site at *MillionDollarPartnering.com* to sign up for free updates.

I look forward to hearing from you and reading your reviews!
Sohail Khan

ABOUT THE AUTHORS

 Jay Conrad Levinson is the author of the best-selling marketing series in history, "Guerrilla Marketing", plus 57 other business books. His books have sold 20 million copies worldwide. And his guerrilla concepts have influenced marketing so much that his books appear in 60 languages and are required reading in MBA programs worldwide.

Jay taught guerrilla marketing for 10 years at the University of California in Berkeley. He was a practitioner of it in the US—as Senior VP at J.Walter Thompson, and in Europe, as Creative Director of Leo Burnett Advertising.

He has been part of the creative teams that made household names of many of the most famous brands in history including: The Marlboro Man and The Pilsbury Doughboy.

Jay sadly passed away on October 10th 2013 (a few weeks after this book was completed) and was the Chairman of Guerrilla Marketing International and the Guerrilla Marketing Association. He transformed so many lives and businesses as the Father of Guerrilla Marketing

You can contact Jay's office at:

JayView@aol.com or www.GMarketing.com

 **Sohail Khan** is the world's premier 'Joint Venture Business Expert' founder of 'The Joint Venture Group' and creator of the 'Million Dollar Partnering System'. A sought after Business Growth Speaker, Author and Marketing Consultant, Sohail works with Corporates, SME's and Educational establishments worldwide.

Known as 'The Joint Venture Expert'.

Sohail has over 15 years' delivering premier training and consulting on the topic of joint ventures and business growth.

Sohail is in demand as a keynote speaker, consultant and facilitator in the areas of marketing, business growth, joint ventures and leadership. His high impact speeches, seminars and bootcamps have received rave reviews and standing ovations worldwide.

Sohail has a Masters' Degree in International Business, is a Certified Guerrilla Marketing Coach/Trainer and a Prince 2 Certified Project Management Practitioner.

To contact Sohail about booking him to speak or do a LIVE joint venture at your event, consulting, coaching or even train your entire team please contact him at:

sohail@sohail-khan.com or www.Sohail-Khan.com

CPSIA information can be obtained at www.ICGtesting.com
Printed in the USA
BVOW07*0611231014

371912BV00054B/433/P